Cambridge
First
Practice Tests

Five tests for the Cambridge English: First *exam*

MARK HARRISON

OXFORD
UNIVERSITY PRESS

ACKNOWLEDGEMENTS

*The author and publisher are grateful to those who have given permission to reproduce
the following extracts and adaptations of copyright material:*

p.6 Extract from 'Multitasking children are losing the plot' by John Elliott,
The Sunday Times, 26 March 2006. Reproduced by permission of NI
Syndication.

p.10 Extract from 'Hi, anxiety' by Tiffany Hancock, The Telegraph, 17
January 2006 www.telegraph.co.uk. © Telegraph Media Group Limited 2006.
Reproduced by permission.

p.12 Extract from 'Want to join the jet set?' by Linda Whitney, The Daily
Mail, 30 March 2006. Reproduced by permission of Solo Syndication.

p.15 Extract adapted from 'The best-seller's book club' by Lesley Jones and
Ophelia Zwart, Eve Magazine, May 2005. Reproduced by permission of
Haymarket Media Group.

p.20 Extract from 'A Life in Sport: The Duke of Argyll Elephant Polo' by
Sarah Edworthy, The Telegraph, 29 November 2006. © Telegraph Media
Group Limited 2006. Reproduced by permission.

p.26 Extract from 'A shopping revolution' by Natasha Perry from p.17,
Hendon & Finchley Times 16 March 2006. Reproduced by permission of
Newsquest London Ltd.

p.30 Adapted from 'A Gathering Light' by Jennifer Donnelly, A&C Black
Publishers, an imprint of Bloomsbury Publishing PLC and 'A Northern Light'
by Jennifer Donnelly. Copyright © 2003 by Jennifer Donnelly. Used by
permission of Houghton Mifflin Harcourt Publishing Company. All rights
reserved.

p.32 Extract from 'The tower and the glory' by Chris Wilson, The Telegraph,
10 September 2005. © Telegraph Media Group Limited 2005. Reproduced by
permission.

p.35 Extract from 'Wheels that changed the world' by Nick Horley, The Daily
Mail, 9 May 2005. Reproduced by permission of Solo Syndication.

p.39 Extract from 'Power to the people' by David Derbyshire, The Telegraph,
4 November 2006. © Telegraph Media Group Limited 2006. Reproduced by
permission.

p.46 Extract from 'See the New Car in the Joneses' Driveway? You May Soon
Be Driving One Just Like It' by David Leonhardt, from The New York Times,
13 June 2005 © 2005 The New York Times. All rights reserved. Used by
permission and protected by the Copyright Laws of the United States. The
printing, copying, redistribution, or retransmission of this Content without
express written permission is prohibited.

p.50 Extract from 'Are you on the right track? How to find a career that
fits your personality' by Frances Childs, The Telegraph, 18 August 2005.
© Telegraph Media Group Limited 2005. Reproduced by permission.

p.52 Extract from 'Strike out with street fighting class' from p.15 Hendon
& Finchley Times 9 March 2006. Reproduced by permission of Newsquest
London Ltd.

p.55 Extract from 'Smart art' by Sean Newson in The Sunday Times, 19 June
2005. Reproduced by permission of NI Syndication.

p.62 Extract from 'Our girls are alive with the *Sound of Music*' by Hugh Davies,
The Telegraph 14 October 2006. © Telegraph Media Group Limited 2006.
Reproduced by permission.

p.66 Extract from 'She's Studying. He's Playing' by John Schwartz, The New
York Times, 14 June 2005 © 2005 The New York Times. All rights reserved.
Used by permission and protected by the Copyright Laws of the United
States. The printing, copying, redistribution, or retransmission of this
Content without express written permission is prohibited.

p.68 Extract from 'Itineraries; Grading the C.E.O. Speech' by Sharon
McDonnell, The New York Times, 27 September 2005 © 2005 The New
York Times. All rights reserved. Used by permission and protected by the
Copyright Laws of the United States. The printing, copying, redistribution,
or retransmission of this Content without express written permission is
prohibited.

p.70 Extract from 'Why I've taken a break from holidays' by Tom Cox,
The Telegraph 18 August 2005. © Telegraph Media Group Limited 2005.
Reproduced by permission.

p.72 Extract from 'Please Don't Touch the Celebrities' by Patricia Leigh
Brown, The New York Times, 2 March 2006 © 2006 The New York Times. All
rights reserved. Used by permission and protected by the Copyright Laws of
the United States. The printing, copying, redistribution, or retransmission of
this Content without express written permission is prohibited.

p.75 Extract from 'Baseball's Origins: They Ain't Found Till They're Found'
by Bill Pennington, The New York Times, 12 September 2004 © 2004 The
New York Times. All rights reserved. Used by permission and protected
by the Copyright Laws of the United States. The printing, copying,
redistribution, or retransmission of this Content without express written
permission is prohibited.

p.78 Extract from '24 Hours in Food' by Kate Salter, The Sunday Times,
September 2006. Reproduced by permission of NI Syndication.

p.78 Adapted extract from 'Piers Morgan meets … Johnny Depp,' Issue 29
17–23 November 2006 www.FirstNews.co.uk. Reproduced by permission of
FirstNews.

p.79 Extract from 'Dashboard dunces exposed' by Sally Pook, The Telegraph
3 March 2006. © Telegraph Media Group Limited 2006. Reproduced by
permission.

p.80 Extract from 'Change your life in 60 seconds' by Louise Armistead, The
Sunday Times, 19 June 2005. Reproduced by permission of NI Syndication.

p.82 Extract from "You can CY" Taken from Angel Magazine July 2006, www.
angelmagazine.co.uk. Reproduced by permission of Archant Community
Media Ltd.

*Although every effort has been made to trace and contact copyright holders before
publication, this has not been possible in some cases. We apologise for any apparent
infringement of copyright and, if notified, the publisher will be pleased to rectify any
errors or omissions at the earliest possible opportunity.*

*The publisher would like to thank the following for their kind permission to
reproduce photographs:* Alamy pp.12 (XiXinXing), 24 (Modern house/Gregg
Vignal), 24 (Girl/OlegMit), 24 (Boys/RichardBaker), 44 (Skyfall/Photos 12),
55 (Archivart), 64 (Graduates/Blend Images), 72 (Arcaid Images), 84 (Coach/
John Powell Photographer), 84 (Backpackers/Andrew Woodley); 84 (Working
from home/Tetra Images), Getty Images pp.24 (Messy room/Photofusion),
52 (tunart), 64 (Business people/A. Chederros), 64 (Businessmen/Stockbyte),
75 (Skip ODonnell), 84 (Modern office/Nick David); Oxford University Press
pp.44 (Professional kitchen/Oxford University Press), 44 (Family cooking/
Karina Mansfield); Rex Features p.44 (Escape from Planet Earth/Snap Stills);
shutterstock pp.34 (KarSol), 64 (Tourist/Ekaterina Pokrovsky); The Random
House Group Ltd. p.15 (Jeff Cottenden)
Tables on pp.94 and 95 reproduced with permission of Cambridge English
Language Assessment © 2014

Contents

Introduction

This book contains:

- four print practice tests for the Cambridge English: First exam (2015)
- access to a complete online practice test
- answer key, including mark schemes for all Writing tasks
- model answers for all Writing tasks
- guidance on how to assess the Writing and Speaking papers
- answer sheets
- audio scripts

Exam content

Reading and Use of English (1 hour 15 minutes)

	Text / Input	Question type	Focus
PART 1	1 short text with 8 gaps	4-option multiple-choice; choose the correct word(s) to fill each gap	vocabulary (e.g. idioms, collocations, completion of phrases, phrasal verbs, etc.) 8 questions; 8 marks
PART 2	1 short text with 8 gaps	fill each gap with one word	mostly grammar, some vocabulary 8 questions; 8 marks
PART 3	1 short text with 8 gaps	use the words given to form the correct word for each gap	word formation 8 questions; 8 marks
PART 4	6 unrelated sentences, each followed by a single word and a gapped sentence	use the word given to complete the gapped sentence so that it means the same as the first sentence	grammar, vocabulary, collocation 6 questions; 12 marks *(each correct answer receives up to 2 marks)*
PART 5	1 text	4-option multiple choice	comprehension of detail, opinion, attitude, purpose, gist, meaning from context, implication, reference, exemplification, main idea, tone 6 questions; 12 marks
PART 6	1 text with 6 sentences missing	choice of 7 sentences to fill the gaps	understanding of text structure, links between parts of text, global meaning 6 questions; 12 marks
PART 7	1 text divided into sections OR several short texts	matching statements / information to section of text or short text they refer to or appear in	comprehension of specific information, detail, opinion, implication 10 questions; 10 marks

Writing (1 hour 20 minutes)

	Task	Focus
PART 1	essay, responding to given title and using given ideas and an idea of their own for content (140–190 words) Candidates **must** do this task.	expressing and giving reasons for an opinion
PART 2	article, report, review, email or letter (140–190 words) Candidates choose one task from three choices.	varying according to the task, including advising, comparing, describing, explaining, expressing opinions, justifying, recommending

Listening (40 minutes)

In the exam, each recording is heard twice. On the CD, Parts 2, 3 and 4 are not repeated and the track will need to be played again. At the end of the exam, candidates are given 5 minutes to transfer their answers to the answer sheet.

	Recording	Question type	Focus
PART 1	8 short pieces (monologue or conversation)	3-option multiple-choice (1 question per piece)	genre, identifying speaker feeling, attitude, opinion, purpose, agreement between speakers, gist, detail **8 questions; 8 marks**
PART 2	1 monologue	sentence completion: 10 sentences to complete with a word or short phrase	understanding of specific information, detail, stated opinion **10 questions; 10 marks**
PART 3	5 short monologues	matching: match what each speaker says to 1 of 8 options	identifying attitude, opinion, gist, purpose, feeling, main points, detail **5 questions; 5 marks**
PART 4	1 interview or conversation (2 speakers)	3-option multiple-choice	identifying opinion, attitude, detail, gist, main idea, specific information **7 questions; 7 marks**

Speaking (14 minutes)

	Activity type (examiner + two candidates)	Focus
PART 1	conversation between candidates and examiner (2 mins)	general interaction, social language
PART 2	individual 'long turn' for each candidate with a brief response from second candidate (4 mins)	comparing, describing, expressing opinions
PART 3	2-way conversation between candidates (4 mins)	exchanging ideas, expressing and justifying opinions, agreeing/disagreeing, suggesting, speculating, evaluating, negotiating
PART 4	conversation between candidates and examiner (4 mins)	expressing and justifying opinions, agreeing/disagreeing, speculating

The Reading and Use of English paper carries 40% of the total. The Writing, Listening and Speaking papers each carry 20% of the total.

Reading and Use of English (1 hour 15 minutes)

<u>PART 1</u>

For questions 1–8, read the text below and decide which answer (A, B, C or D) best fits each gap. There is an example at the beginning (0).

Mark your answers on the separate answer sheet.

Example:

0 A seriously   **B** extremely   **C** absolutely   **D** intensely

0	**A**	**B**	**C**	**D**

Multitasking children

The trend for children to multitask by juggling all sorts of electronic gadgets at the same time is **0**_____ damaging their levels of concentration, scientists have warned. They found that children **1**_____ homework while sending messages via the Internet can **2**_____ up spending 50% longer than if they had done each task **3**_____ .

David E Meyer, Professor of Cognitive Psychology at the University of Michigan, said that true multitasking is **4**_____ possible for simple activities such as ironing and listening to the radio. He ran experiments demonstrating that young adults who had to **5**_____ from one maths problem to another wasted significant amounts of time. Meyer said: 'For situations **6**_____ more complex tasks, especially those requiring language, the total time taken to get all the tasks done will increase **7**_____ . Over long periods, this kind of multitasking can stress you out and **8**_____ to mental and physical exhaustion.'

1	**A** engaging	**B** tackling	**C** attending	**D** undergoing
2	**A** turn	**B** come	**C** use	**D** end
3	**A** separately	**B** distinctly	**C** apart	**D** aside
4	**A** merely	**B** purely	**C** only	**D** simply
5	**A** alter	**B** switch	**C** interrupt	**D** exchange
6	**A** consisting	**B** containing	**C** involving	**D** meaning
7	**A** largely	**B** greatly	**C** widely	**D** highly
8	**A** result	**B** proceed	**C** lead	**D** bring

PART 2

For questions 9–16, read the text below and think of the word which best fits each gap. Use only one word in each gap. There is an example at the beginning (0).

Write your answers IN CAPITAL LETTERS *on the separate answer sheet.*

Example:

0	I	T											

The London Marathon

The London Marathon race is a long-running story. **0** _____ was first held in 1981,

9 _____ when more than half a million marathon runners of various shapes, sizes and abilities have completed the challenge of running the full 42 km of the course.

The London Marathon was the brainchild of Chris Brasher. The former Olympic champion brought the idea home to London **10** _____ completing the New York Marathon in 1979. 'Could London stage **11** _____ an event?' wondered Brasher, answering his **12** _____ question by organizing the first London Marathon on March 29 1981, **13** _____ 6,255 runners completed the course.

The event has captured the public imagination and there are always **14** _____ many people wanting to take part. Last year **15** _____ amazing 98,500 people applied to run in it, although only 46,500 **16** _____ be accepted.

For those who do take part, the day is about fun, achievement and raising money for charity – with varying degrees of pain!

PART 3

For questions 17–24, read the text below. Use the word given in capitals at the end of some of the lines to form a word that fits in the gap in the same line. There is an example at the beginning (0).

Write your answers IN CAPITAL LETTERS on the separate answer sheet.

Example:

| 0 | N | A | T | I | O | N | A | L | | | | | |

MOBILE LIBRARY'S A WINNER

The city's new mobile library has won an award at a **0**_____ meeting   NATION

of mobile library providers. The award is for the **17**_____ design of   STAND

this new vehicle.

    The new library went into **18**_____ in April and has been very well   SERVE

received by the public. Both visits and loans of books have increased

19_____ since the new vehicle began operating. Comments have   CONSIDER

included 'It's such a friendly-looking library', 'I couldn't wait to look

inside!' and 'Thanks for all the **20**_____ new books.'   WONDER

    The mobile library is an air-conditioned, state-of-the-art vehicle, which is

fully networked for using information technology. The air suspension system

allows the vehicle to be **21**_____ for easy access and ensures   LOW

22_____ when parked. The internal layout was designed with major   STABLE

input from the library staff, who insisted that the décor was bright and

23_____ . The library carries up to 3,000 books, CDs and DVDs for   COLOUR

all ages and **24**_____ , and much of the stock is brand new.   INTERESTED

PART 4

For questions 25–30, complete the second sentence so that it has a similar meaning to the first sentence, using the word given. Do not change the word given. You must use between two and five words, including the word given. Here is an example (0).

Example:

0   Making new friends was easy for her.

DIFFICULT

She didn't _____ new friends.

The gap can be filled with the words 'find it difficult to make', so you write:

0	F I N D I T D I F F I C U L T T O M A K E

Write only *the missing words* IN CAPITAL LETTERS *on the separate answer sheet.*

---

25   Despite winning the race, he wasn't very pleased.

EVEN

He wasn't very pleased, _____ the race.

26   His first novel was better than this one.

GOOD

This novel is not _____ one he wrote.

27   I'm sorry, could you wait for a moment, please?

MIND

I'm sorry, _____ for a moment, please?

28   We're so late now that we definitely won't get to the party on time.

CHANCE

We're so late that we have _____ to the party on time.

29   The food she eats affects her health badly.

EFFECT

The food she eats _____ her health.

30   The only thing I did at the weekend was housework.

APART

I did _____ housework at the weekend.

PART 5

You are going to read a newspaper article about an adventure centre. For questions 31–36, choose the answer (A, B, C or D) which you think fits best according to the text.

Mark your answers on the separate answer sheet.

A family adventure centre

I'm focused. Completely terrified, but focused. I've got a tiny area to stand on and beneath me is a 10-metre drop. To make things worse, the totem pole that I'm trying to climb onto is shaking. With one knee bent on the top of the pole and the other foot next to it, I slowly stand up with my arms outstretched for balance. Once upright, my legs are still wobbling but an enormous smile has spread across my face. I shuffle my toes over the edge. And then I jump. Back on the ground, my knees won't stop quaking. But for the boys at Head 4 Heights, an aerial adventure centre in Cirencester, it's all in a day's work.

Head 4 Heights, one of the tallest climbing centres in Britain, opened two years ago. It's the only UK climbing centre open to the public year-round (the only days it closes are when winds exceed 70 mph, almost enough to blow you off a totem pole and into one of the lakes). The course was set up by Rod Baber, adventurer extraordinaire and holder of the world record for scaling the highest peak of every country in Europe in the shortest time. Rod's latest plan is to snag the record for North and South America as well, but in between he starts every day with a clamber round the Cirencester course.

Although the course is only roughly the size of a tennis court, it packs a lot into a small space. There are four totem poles (of varying degrees of difficulty according to the holds attached to them), a stairway to heaven (a giant ladder with an increasing distance between the rungs), two freefall platforms and a trapeze jump. Plans for a new 30-metre pole are presently under way. All can be made easier or harder, according to ability, and incorporated into different challenges, which is why the course has proved a success with families, corporate days out and the armed forces. More than half who visit return for more and the centre now averages about 1,500 visitors a month.

All ages over five are welcome, but children are the most enthusiastic and 'far easier to teach than the bankers,' says Rod. Parents are usually more reluctant to join in. 'We hear all sorts of excuses,' says Rod. 'Everything from bad knees to "I haven't trimmed my toenails".' The oldest customer was a 78-year-old who arrived with his son and grandson. When the younger two decided to give it a miss, the grandfather set off to show them how it was done.

For the most part, though, people start off nervous and only gain confidence as they progress. 'Everything is kept very positive. We always tell people to look up not down and to take their time,' says Rod. 'We want to push people outside their comfort zone and into the adventure zone, but we don't want people to be pushed into the panic zone, which can be mentally damaging.'

Also reassuring is the 100 per cent safety record. The course was designed and built by Nick Moriarty, an expert in his field who has constructed 450 courses in 16 countries and trained 2,700 instructors. Key to the design is the safety-rope system, which ensures that if you do lose your balance or grip, your full-body harness will guarantee that you float, not fall, back to earth.

31 One problem the writer describes in the first paragraph is that
    A she keeps falling off the totem pole.
    B she is trying to stand on top of a moving object.
    C she cannot get her arms into the right position.
    D she is too nervous to complete the climb.

31

32 What do we learn about Head 4 Heights in the second paragraph?
    A It remains open even in quite windy conditions.
    B Rod Baber got the idea for it while climbing mountains.
    C It did not initially stay open throughout the year.
    D It is aimed at people who don't have the chance to climb mountains.

32

33 The writer says that the main reason for the course's popularity is that
    A the challenges it offers cannot be found anywhere else.
    B new challenges are constantly being added.
    C it can be completed in a fairly short time.
    D it can be adapted for different people.

33

34 The people who 'decided to give it a miss' (column 3) are examples of people who
    A find it difficult to do the course.
    B are unwilling to do the course.
    C are easily taught how to do the course.
    D give up while they are doing course.

34

35 Rod says that the intention of the course is that people taking part
    A learn how to deal with extreme fear.
    B progress as quickly as possible.
    C take risks they might not initially want to take.
    D increase in confidence after repeated visits.

35

36 The writer uses the phrase 'Also reassuring' (column 3) to emphasize
    A that people benefit from doing the course.
    B how carefully the course has been constructed.
    C that people should not be afraid to do the course.
    D how enthusiastic Rod is about the course.

36

PART 6

You are going to read an article about jobs that involve international travel. Six sentences have been removed from the article. Choose from the sentences A–G the one which fits each gap (37–42). There is one extra sentence which you do not need to use.

Mark your answers on the separate answer sheet.

WANT TO JOIN THE JET SET?

You could be jetting off to exotic locations, staying in five-star hotels, eating in top-class restaurants, and it's all paid for by your employer. Who wouldn't want a job that involves foreign travel? **37**_____ The number of jobs requiring international travel is growing significantly. And citing business travel experience on your CV can bring enormous professional benefits.

But it's not always as exciting as it sounds. There is a big difference between travelling to Milan as a tourist and travelling there to spend a day in the type of hotel meeting room that can be found anywhere in Europe. It can be very exciting, but you need to keep your feet firmly on the ground. **38**_____ Flights can be delayed, things can go wrong and it's easy to get exhausted. Many jobs mean travelling alone, so you can be lonely.

Simply targeting any job that involves foreign travel is not the way to start. Instead, you should consider all the usual factors, such as qualifications and experience, and only then choose a sector or company that offers opportunities for international travel. The travel and hotel trades are obvious areas, but the commercial sector also offers good prospects for travel. In the retail sector, buyers often travel, especially if they work in fresh produce, where they have to check the suitability of crops. **39**_____ Jobs in the engineering and environment sector can involve travel, too. Almost any career can mean international travel, if you choose the right company and role. The number of jobs involving travel, especially at middle-management level, is growing.

So what will help you secure a role with an

international flavour? **40**_____ A second language is a good indication of how well someone will adapt. You need to show you are flexible and willing to learn. If your company has a sister company in the Czech Republic, for instance, learning some Czech will boost your chances.

Find out what the company offers as a support package. Many now guarantee that you can return home at the weekends, or they will limit the amount that people travel each year. **41**_____ One company asked graduates fresh out of university to move to another country over a weekend, alone, and to find their own accommodation.

And it's as well to remember that international travel can be stressful. People can get burned out by international business travel. You need to be in control of your schedule, rather than leaving it to the company. You must ensure you get time to rest and talk to your employer all the time about how you are coping. Don't wait for formal appraisals or until they ask for your views. **42**_____ Most sensible companies ask people to commit to two to three years. This increases the likelihood of success. And most people who travel on business remember it fondly.

A   On the other hand, it does bring personal benefits, and it also has a dramatic effect on promotion prospects.

B   And realize you might not want to travel for ever.

C   Employers look for candidates with an international outlook.

D   And there are plenty of opportunities.

E   But not all employers are like this.

F   Speak to seasoned international business travellers to get an idea of what you will face.

G   Employment in communications, banking and finance, and property management is also worth looking at.

You are going to read a magazine article about various authors. For questions 43–52, choose from the authors (A–D). The authors may be chosen more than once.

Mark your answers on the separate answer sheet.

Which author

took action in response to someone's negative view of her chances of getting her work accepted?	43
decides when information given in her books does not have to be true?	44
did something dishonest while trying to get her work accepted?	45
was offered her first contract as a result of an earlier success?	46
makes sure that her books contain strange elements?	47
draws attention to the likelihood of a new author getting their work accepted?	48
wants people to be cheered up by her books?	49
feels that it is an advantage that people give her their sincere views on her work?	50
recommends analysing various aspects of other authors' books?	51
felt that her job was taking up too much of her attention?	52

The best-sellers book club

Fancy being an author? We asked some of Britain's favourite best-selling writers to share the secrets of their success.

A JOANNE HARRIS *Her novels have attracted millions of fans worldwide.*

MY BIG BREAK I was a full-time teacher and made time to write my first novel before and after school. It took two years. Then I spent a fortune on posting manuscripts to agents. I found one, but he got discouraged when my manuscripts were rejected, so I sacked him and wrote my next novel, which my next agent loved. He got me a deal for both novels.

MY BEST ADVICE 100,000 titles are published in the UK every year. For each, 100 are rejected. If, knowing this, you still want to write and you love it, you're on the right track.

THE SECRET OF MY SUCCESS I don't believe in a magic wand. You need ability, luck and hard work.

B LAUREN CHILD *She writes and illustrates children's books for 2 to 10-year-olds.*

MY BIG BREAK After school, I did an art course. Then I did all sorts of jobs – making lampshades, working as an assistant to artist Damien Hirst (I painted a lot of the spots on his paintings). I wrote my first book in the hope it would become an animation. I found an agent, but didn't get a deal for five years. I didn't lose heart, as so many people were positive about it. Eventually I got a deal and was asked to do a second book.

MY BEST ADVICE Read as much as you can before you even think of writing. And you can't please everyone – above all, your work must interest you.

THE SECRET OF MY SUCCESS I keep stories simple, but always add a quirky touch – children really like the more bizarre moments in life. I also have a very honest audience who tell me what they think.

C FREYA NORTH *She writes lively, fast-paced fiction.*

MY BIG BREAK I was doing a PhD in Art History and bought a computer. The sheer joy of typing then deleting stuff was compulsive and I started to write fiction that I actually wanted to read. After four years of rejections, I presumed I was doing something wrong. Then I worked for a publishing company and realized I needed an agent. I sent my manuscript with fake reviews I'd made up myself to lots of agents. One took me on and got me a three-book deal.

MY BEST ADVICE Let your character dictate the story. It could be the most intricate plot in the world, but if the characters aren't 'real', no one will care.

THE SECRET OF MY SUCCESS I write simply and keep chapters short so my readers can enjoy them on journeys home at the end of a bad day. I want them to giggle.

D MANDA SCOTT *She has written a cult series of historical novels.*

MY BIG BREAK I was a veterinary anaesthetist. On my 30th birthday, I was climbing a mountain and I was happy, but all I could think about was work on Monday. I decided to follow my heart and make a living from writing. I was among the finalists in a writing competition and from that got a deal for my first book.

MY BEST ADVICE Read bad books and work out what makes them bad. Read the books you love and work out why you love them. Write what you will really, really want to read. Always.

THE SECRET OF MY SUCCESS I'm good at judging what needs to be factual and what I can make up.

Writing (1 hour 20 minutes)

PART 1

*You **must** answer this question. Write your answer in 140–190 words in an appropriate style.*

1 In your English class you have been talking about computer games and the effects they have on people who play them. Now, your English teacher has asked you to write an essay.

Write an essay using **all** the notes and give reasons for your point of view.

> Computer games are very bad for people and they cause a lot of problems.
> Do you agree?
>
> Notes
> Write about:
> 1.   time spent playing the games
> 2.   feelings they give to people
> 3.   _____ (your own idea)

PART 2

Write an answer to one of the questions 2–4 in this part. Write your answer in 140–190 words in an appropriate style.

2   You are going to visit Britain for three weeks in the near future. You have received an email from a British friend, Olivia. Read this part of Olivia's email and then write your email to Mr and Mrs Hampson.

> While you're here, you could stay with some relatives of mine (Joe and Lisa Hampson) who live in the Midlands. I've spoken to them and they'd be pleased to put you up for a few days. I think you should write to them (address below), tell them about yourself and your plans, and ask for information about what you can do there.

Write your **email**.

3   You have seen this announcement in an international magazine.

> ### PERFORMING IN PUBLIC
>
> Tell us about your experience of performing or speaking in public. What did you do and where? How did it go? Was it a success or a disaster? And how did you feel?
>
> We'll publish the best articles in a special section next month.

Write your **article**.

4   You recently saw this notice in an English-language magazine.

> ### WHAT DON'T YOU LIKE ON TV?
>
> Is there a programme on TV that you really dislike? We're looking for reviews of programmes you really can't stand. Tell us what you don't like about the programme and we'll publish the angriest reviews!

Write your **review**.

Listening (40 minutes)

PART 1

You will hear people talking in eight different situations. For questions 1–8, choose the best answer, (A, B or C).

1 You hear someone talking about football referees.
   What is the speaker's attitude towards referees?

   A They make too many mistakes.

   B They deserve sympathy.   `1`

   C Some are better than others.

2 You hear a famous chef talking about his week.
   What does he say about what happened during the week?

   A He had a problem that was not his fault.

   B He didn't want to appear on so many programmes.   `2`

   C He had his first experience of live TV.

3 You hear someone talking about her career in dancing.
   What does she emphasize?

   A the contribution made by her parents

   B how much hard work she did   `3`

   C her desire to be a dancer

4 You hear someone talking on the phone at work.
   Who is she talking to?

   A a colleague

   B her boss   `4`

   C a client

5   You hear a radio presenter talking about a book.
    What feeling does the presenter express about the book?

    A   doubt that it does exactly what it says it does

    B   amazement at how up to date its information is   5

    C   curiosity about how it was written

6   You hear part of an interview with a famous comedian.
    What does he say about his school days?

    A   The teachers never criticized him.

    B   He was only good at one subject.   6

    C   Other people found him amusing.

7   You hear someone talking about a person he knows.
    What is the speaker doing?

    A   complaining

    B   apologizing   7

    C   arguing

8   You hear a tour guide talking to a group of visitors to a museum.
    What does he tell them about the museum?

    A   It's easy to get lost in it.

    B   Big groups aren't allowed in some parts of it.   8

    C   It's better only to visit a small part of it.

PART 2

You will hear someone talking about the sport of elephant polo. For questions 9–18, complete the sentences with a word or short phrase.

ELEPHANT POLO

Elephants are 9 _____ animals and so they enjoy elephant polo.

The 10 _____ of a goal in elephant polo is the same as in football.

A player and an elephant 11 _____ both sit on each elephant.

It is against the rules for the elephants to use their trunks to

12 _____ the ball.

A total of 13 _____ elephants are required for a game to take place.

The participants are in action for a total of 14 _____ during each game.

The stick used in the game is both 15 _____ and _____ .

The elephants sometimes want to 16 _____ in front of a goal.

An elephant with a bad 17 _____ will be taken out of a game.

African elephants are not used because 18 _____ cause a problem.

PART 3

You will hear five different people talking about cities they have visited. For questions 19–23, choose from the list (A–H) the opinion each person gives about the city. Use the letters only once. There are three extra letters which you do not need to use.

A   It was exactly as I had imagined.

Speaker 1   19

B   It is not as good as it used to be.

Speaker 2   20

C   It is smaller than I had thought.

Speaker 3   21

D   It is hard to find your way around it.

Speaker 4   22

E   It is overrated.

Speaker 5   23

F   It is better for a long visit than a short one.

G   It can get too crowded.

H   It was even better than I expected.

PART 4

You will hear an interview with someone who is involved in the music business. For questions 24–30, choose the best answer (A, B or C).

24 What does James say about the radio station he started?

    A Its name was very appropriate.

    B It was more popular than he had expected.   24

    C It was not very expensive to run.

25 What does James say about people's attitudes towards his age?

    A They were nicer to him when he was 12 than when he was 16.

    B They were more jealous of him when he was 12 than when he was 16.   25

    C They expected more of him when he was 16 than when he was 12.

26 James says that his career in music has included

    A taking over a local radio station.

    B making advertisements.   26

    C setting up new festivals.

27 What do we learn about advertising on James' TV channel?

    A There isn't any of it.

    B It always includes music.   27

    C It doesn't interrupt the programmes.

28 What does James say about the people interviewed on the channel?

    A They have to say something interesting.

    B They enjoy being interviewed.   28

    C They often say unexpected things.

29 What does James say about his ideas?

    A Some of them are not very realistic.

    B He expects to have good ones all the time.   29

    C He makes sure that he doesn't forget them.

30 James's advice to listeners who might want to go into business is to

    A forget about past problems.

    B learn from past mistakes.   30

    C take big risks.

Speaking (14 minutes)

PART 1 (2 minutes)

Where you live

- Where do you live?

- How long have you been living there?

- What kind of building do you live in?

- What do you like / dislike about the town / village / district where you live?

Travel

- Have you been to many other countries? ..... (Which ones?)

- Would you like to travel more? ..... (Where?)

- What's the best country / city / region that you've visited? ..... (Why?)

- Which country / city / region would you most like to visit? ..... (Why?)

School

- What is / was your favourite school subject? ...... (Why?)

- Describe one of your school friends.

- Which school subject(s) do / did you most dislike? ...... (Why?)

- Describe a teacher at your school.

PART 2 (4 minutes)

1 Outdoor activities
2 People's rooms

Candidate A	Look at the two photographs 1A and 1B on page 24. They show people doing outdoor activities. Compare the photographs and say what the people are trying to do. *Candidate A talks on his / her own for about 1 minute.*
Candidate B	Which of the activities would you prefer to do, and why? *Candidate B talks on his / her own for about 30 seconds.*
Candidate B	Look at the two photographs 2A and 2B on page 24. They show people's rooms. Compare the photographs and say whose rooms they might be. *Candidate B talks on his / her own for about 1 minute.*
Candidate A	Which of the rooms is most similar to yours, and in what ways? *Candidate A talks on his / her own for about 30 seconds.*

PART 2

■ What are the people trying to do?

1A

1B

■ Whose rooms do you think these are?

2A

2B

PARTS 3 AND 4 (8 minutes)

Exhibitions for a museum

PART 3 (4 minutes)

Imagine that a local museum is trying to increase visitor numbers. Look at the ideas for new exhibitions that are being considered by the museum.

First, talk to each other about how popular each of the suggestions would be.

Then decide which two would attract the most visitors to the museum.

Candidates A and B discuss this together for about 3 minutes.

PART 4 (4 minutes)

- Do you like going to museums or art galleries? ..... (Why / Why not?)
- Which of the subjects interests you the most and which interests you the least? ..... (Why?)
- What are the most well-known museums or art galleries in the place you come from? What do they have in them?
- What kind of things do museums offer to attract young people?
- What is the most interesting museum or art gallery that you've been to? ...... (Why?)
- Which museum or art gallery would you most like to visit? Where is it? What does it have in it? What would you like to see there? ..... (Why?)
- Some people think that museums and art galleries are boring. Do you agree?

Reading and Use of English (1 hour 15 minutes)

<u>PART 1</u>

For questions 1–8, read the text below and decide which answer (A, B, C or D) best fits each gap. There is an example at the beginning (0).

Mark your answers on the separate answer sheet.

Example:

0 **A** estimated   **B** awaited   **C** assessed   **D** predicted

0	A	B	C	D

Britain's first shopping centre

When Brent Cross Shopping Centre in London opened it was the first large-scale indoor shopping centre in Britain and many people **0**_____ it would be a **1**_____ failure. Instead, the centre, with its 75 stores, started a shopping **2** _____ in Britain.

'They said it **3**_____ no chance of becoming popular, but in the first week it was packed, and that's how it's **4**_____ on,' said George Dorman, who has been working as a fruit and vegetable sales assistant at the Waitrose store since it opened. It's a **5**_____ achievement and 'I've enjoyed every **6**_____ minute of it,' he said.

Sisters Jeanette Harris and Lydia Neidus have both been working as sales assistants at the Fenwicks store since the centre opened. Ms Neidus said: 'The more you get involved, the more you love it because you've seen everything and you've **7**_____ so much knowledge about it all.' Her sister added: 'I **8**_____ as if it was just yesterday when I started and I've loved every minute.'

1	**A** whole	**B** complete	**C** full	**D** true
2	**A** novelty	**B** alteration	**C** conversion	**D** revolution
3	**A** took	**B** stood	**C** ran	**D** held
4	**A** stayed	**B** carried	**C** moved	**D** stuck
5	**A** great	**B** high	**C** large	**D** vast
6	**A** actual	**B** single	**C** individual	**D** separate
7	**A** increased	**B** gained	**C** raised	**D** expanded
8	**A** feel	**B** seem	**C** sense	**D** find

PART 2

For questions 9–16, read the text below and think of the word which best fits each gap. Use only one *word in each gap. There is an example at the beginning (0).*

Write your answers IN CAPITAL LETTERS *on the separate answer sheet.*

Example:

0	H	O	W										

See dinosaurs eating!

Dinosaurs died out more than 60 million years ago, so **0** _____ can we tell what they used to eat? Find out at the Cameron Museum, where you can step **9** _____ in time and join some dinosaurs enjoying their lunch. **10** _____ you enter the new Meet the Dinosaurs exhibition, you'll meet four full-size dinosaur heads, each of them munching away on their favourite food. The model dinosaurs are **11** _____ realistic that you could easily forget that they're not real.

   Scientists have pieced **12** _____ information from fossils to work out that dinosaurs with large claws and sharp teeth ate meat, while flatter teeth were used **13** _____ grinding plants. So Tyrannosaurus rex, with its prehistoric table manners **14** _____ teeth as sharp as razors, might not have been the **15** _____ relaxing dinner guest!

   But, whether you're a meat eater or a vegetarian, **16** _____ not come along to the exhibition and make sure you don't miss an incredible day out!

PART 3

For questions 17–24, read the text below. Use the word given in capitals at the end of some of the lines to form a word that fits in the gap in the same line. There is an example at the beginning (0).

Write your answers IN CAPITAL LETTERS *on the separate answer sheet.*

Example:

| 0 | C | H | A | L | L | E | N | G | I | N | G | | |

ESCORTED TOURS

Organizing a holiday can be a very **0** _____ task. Some people find	CHALLENGE
the experience as **17** _____ as the daily demands of work and family	STRESS
commitments. If you are in this situation, you may find that taking an	
escorted holiday is the ideal **18** _____ .	SOLVE
Escorted holidays offer a great balance between sightseeing, entertainment	
and leisure time, with the added advantage that you have the services of a	
professional tour manager, who **19** _____ you throughout the trip,	COMPANY
acting as your **20** _____ guide. From the first day to the last, tour	PERSON
managers make your holiday experience even more **21** _____ because	MEMORY
of the invaluable information and **22** _____ suggestions they provide.	HELP
Your tour manager will give you many **23** _____ into the place you are	SIGHT
visiting, including useful information on the distinctive characteristics	
of the place, such as regional food and local entertainment.	
If you book one of the escorted holiday packages that we offer, you can be	
sure that you will have a **24** _____ authentic travel experience.	TRUE

PART 4

For questions 25–30, complete the second sentence so that it has a similar meaning to the first sentence, using the word given. Do not change the word given. *You must use between* two *and* five *words, including the word given. Here is an example (0).*

Example:

0   Making new friends was easy for her.

   DIFFICULT

   She didn't _____ new friends.

The gap can be filled with the words 'find it difficult to make', so you write:

0	FIND IT DIFFICULT TO MAKE

Write only *the missing words* IN CAPITAL LETTERS on the separate answer sheet.

25   He didn't buy a present for her, he gave her some money.

   INSTEAD

   He gave her some money _____ present.

26   A temporary manager is running the shop at the moment.

   RUN

   The shop _____ a temporary manager at the moment.

27   How long is your journey from home to work?

   TAKE

   How long _____ get from home to work?

28   When I rang the box office, the tickets had all been sold.

   LEFT

   There _____ when I rang the box office.

29   If public opinion doesn't change suddenly, he'll win the next election.

   SUDDEN

   Unless _____ change in public opinion, he'll win the next election.

30   This is the happiest that Paula has ever been.

   HAPPIER

   Paula _____ she is now.

You are going to read an extract from a novel. For questions 31–36, choose the answer (A, B, C or D) which you think fits best according to the text.

Mark your answers on the separate answer sheet.

The Fulton Chain Floating Library is only a tiny room, a closet really, below decks in Charlie Eckler's pickle boat. It is nothing like the proper library they have in Old Forge, but it has its own element of surprise. Mr Eckler uses the room to store his wares, and when he finally gets around to moving a chest of tea or a sack of cornmeal, you never know what you might find. And once in a while, the main library in Herkimer sends up a new book or two. It's nice to get your hands on a new book before everyone else does. While the pages are still clean and white and the spine hasn't been snapped.

I stepped onto the boat and went below decks. The *House of Mirth* was under *W*, like Mr Eckler said it would be, only it was wedged next to *Mrs Wiggs of the Cabbage Patch*. Mr Eckler sometimes gets authors and titles confused. I signed it out in a ledger he kept on top of a molasses barrel, then rooted around behind a crate of eggs, a jar of marbles and a box of dried dates but found nothing I hadn't already read. I remembered to get the bag of cornmeal we needed. I wished I could buy oatmeal or white flour instead, but cornmeal cost less and went further. I was to get a ten-pound bag. The fifty-pound bag cost more to buy but was cheaper per pound and I'd told Pa so, but he said only rich people can afford to be thrifty.

Just as I was about to climb back upstairs, something caught my eye – a box of composition books. Real pretty ones with hard covers on them, and swirly paint designs, and a ribbon to mark your place. I put the cornmeal down, and Mrs Wharton too, and picked one up. Its pages were smooth and white. I thought it would be a fine thing to write on paper that nice. The pages in my old composition book were rough and had blurry blue lines printed on them, and were made with so little care that there were slivers of wood visible in them.

I handed Mr Eckler fifty cents of my father's money for the cornmeal. 'How much is this?' I asked, holding up one of the pretty composition books. I had sixty cents from all the fiddleheads Weaver and I had sold to the Eagle Bay Hotel. It was money I knew I should have given to my pa. I'd meant to, really. I just hadn't gotten around to it.

'Those notebooks? They're expensive, Mattie. Italians made them. I've got to get forty-five cents apiece,' he said. 'I've got some others coming in for fifteen cents in a week or so if you can wait.'

Forty-five cents was a good deal of money, but I didn't want the ones for fifteen cents, not after I'd seen the others. I had ideas. Tons of them. For stories and poems. I chewed the inside of my cheek, deliberating. I knew I would have to write a lot when I went to Barnard College– if I went to Barnard College – and it might be a good idea to get a head start. Weaver had said I should be using my words, not just collecting them, and I knew they would just glide across this beautiful paper, and when I was done writing them, I could close them safely inside the covers. Just like a real book. Guilt gnawed at my insides. I took the money from my pocket and gave it to Mr Eckler quickly, so the thing was done and I couldn't change my mind.

31 What does Mattie say about the library in Mr Eckler's boat?
    A New books are frequently added to it.
    B All the books in it are in excellent condition.
    C It contains books that are hidden from view.
    D Mr Eckler doesn't know exactly what is in it.

32 When Mattie found the new book, she
    A discovered that there were other new books nearby.
    B saw that it had been put in the wrong place.
    C followed Mr Eckler's system for borrowing books.
    D had to move something so that she could find it.

33 What was the situation concerning the cornmeal?
    A Her father was unable to save money by buying the bigger bag.
    B Her father could not see the point of buying the bigger bag.
    C Her father felt that cornmeal was better than oatmeal or white flour.
    D Her father had decided to stop buying what he usually bought.

34 One reason why Mattie liked the look of the composition books was that
    A the covers were shiny.
    B the pages were completely clear.
    C the pages were thicker than in her old book.
    D they had better ribbons than her old book.

35 When Mattie asked Mr Eckler how much the composition books cost, he said that
    A they weren't really worth the money.
    B they were not the books he had been expecting to receive.
    C he did not expect many people to buy them.
    D he had no choice about how much to charge for them.

36 While she was buying one of the books, Mattie thought about
    A how she could use it for making lists of words.
    B what the experience of writing in it would be like.
    C what people at Barnard College would think of it.
    D whether she would have enough ideas to fill the whole book.

You are going to read an article about an activity in Spain. Six sentences have been removed from the article. Choose from the sentences A–G the one which fits each gap (37–42). There is one extra sentence which you do not need to use.

Mark your answers on the separate answer sheet.

The Tower and the Glory

Chris Wilson starts at the bottom when he joins a Spanish team making competitive human pyramids

A large man jams his foot in my ear and jumps on to my shoulders. He is quickly followed by another only slightly smaller gentleman who grabs my belt and shimmies up me like a pole. Another follows. My face contorts with pain as the fourth tier mounts on to my back and I begin to sway dangerously. **37**_____.

'Castelling' (making human castles) is a family sport in Catalonia. Groups normally consist of everyone from tiny children, through awkward adolescents and wiry women, to well-built men at the bottom. **38**_____ I had also heard that being overweight and unfit would not count against me. Sure enough, when I turned up for my first training session, I could sense that, for the first time in years, my ever-expanding physique was being appreciatively looked at.

Castelling began almost 200 years ago near Tarragona, just south of Barcelona. Out of nowhere, it seems that people suddenly began forming themselves into human towers. Since then the sport, if you can call it that, has become an expression

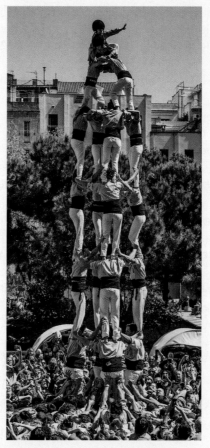

of Catalan identity, with groups competing to build ever higher and more elegant structures.

39_____ Once or twice it has managed a six-tier tower. The top teams regularly manage eight or nine. It was my intention to add a little British beef to the group to help them reach the next level in time for the competitions to be held tomorrow in Barcelona on the National Day of Catalonia.

At first I had thought that I might like to go on top to bask in the glory, but the club's president soon put me straight. He indicated a spindly little girl who looked as though she had been raised entirely on broccoli, and not much of it at that. It is she who has pride of place on top of the pyramid. **40**_____ For my first try-out I was given the role of *segones mans* (second hands), which meant that I supported the wrists of the man who supported the buttocks of the first rank of the pyramid.

Once I had assumed my position, people began to scramble up me and on to the tower without warning. **41**_____ Still, my hard work must have been appreciated because I was quickly promoted to be *primeres mans* and support the bottoms of the first level of the pyramid that we were making under the watchful eye of the artistic director.

My performance in the 'hands' section had obviously been satisfactory because at the third training session I was called forward and given the very great honour of the President's Belt. **42**_____ Being offered this belt, still warm from the very waist of the President, was a clear gesture that me and my bulk had been accepted. Finally, I had made it to the bottom of the pile.

TEST 2

A   The best I could hope for was to be at the bottom, but even that honour has to be earned.

B   So I knew that everyone at the training session that night would have cheered with good-natured delight if I had done that.

C   I had been attracted to castelling because I had been told that it requires almost no skill or co-ordination.

D   Within seconds I had assisted in the formation of a three-tier tower without really noticing what was happening.

E   It's not easy being the bottom man of a human pyramid.

F   Each casteller is wound into a large strip of material worn around the waist to support the back and to help the other castellers grip when they climb.

G   The group I had joined in Figueres, near the French border, is very much a second-division outfit.

PART 7

You are going to read a magazine article about the history of the bicycle. For questions 43–52, choose from the sections of the article (A–D). The sections may be chosen more than once.

Mark your answers on the separate answer sheet.

___

In which section of the article are the following mentioned?

features that were not added because they were considered problematic	43
a design that is exactly the same as that of current products	44
a product that became popular despite its price in comparison with an existing product	45
a warning that affected the appeal of a certain product	46
an attempt to get publicity	47
the possibility of injury because of where the rider sat	48
products that were introduced to compensate for a disadvantage of another product	49
a design that some manufacturers felt would not become popular	50
people riding a certain product in order to impress others	51
the motivation of one set of people for changing bicycle design	52

Wheels that changed the world

A The bicycle was an absolutely extraordinary creation. Inventors had first begun to wrestle with the challenge of coming up with a human-powered vehicle in the 17th century. The beginnings of the modern bicycle emerged in 1818 when Karl von Drais, an eccentric German baron, invented what we now know as the hobbyhorse. It was bicycle-shaped with wooden wheels but had no pedals: the rider had to push it forward with his feet. The hobbyhorse could be afforded only by true gentlemen, and it soon became a much sought-after status symbol. But the craze died out after a year following a statement from the London College of Surgeons, which said darkly that the hobbyhorse could cause 'internal injuries'.

B Brilliant minds continued to wrestle with the mechanical horse but made slow progress. Even Britain's top engineer, Isambard Kingdom Brunel, could come up with nothing better than a hobbyhorse that ran on railway tracks. Finally, in 1887, a Parisian blacksmith called Pierre Michaux added a pair of pedals to a hobbyhorse, and the bicycle was born. The Michaux bicycle had pedals fixed directly to the front wheel, just like a child's tricycle today. Made largely of iron, it weighed as much as a fridge but was easy to ride and took a man up to five miles with the effort he would use to walk only one. Michaux's first newspaper advertisement in May 1867 offered 'pedal velocipedes' for 250 francs. At this price only the wealthy could afford one and a group of 20 young men spent their days showing off their 'steeds' before fascinated crowds in the Bois de Boulogne. Michaux was soon producing 20 bicycles a day, and decided to organize a women's race as a stunt to boost his sales further. Within a year, there were 50,000 bicycles in France.

C Not to be outdone by their French counterparts, British engineers set about improving bicycle design with wire-spoked wheels and solid rubber tyres. Gears and chains were still thought too heavy and complex to be fitted to a bicycle, so designers could increase top speed only by increasing the size of the front wheel. Eventually front wheels grew until they were 5ft and the penny farthing was born. Speeds of 20 mph were now possible, but the rider's seat was directly above the front wheel, which made riding in a skirt impossible, so women were effectively barred from bicycles. To make up for it, manufacturers developed tricycles with low seats. The penny farthing's biggest drawback was its danger: the high seat was difficult to climb into, and once up there the driver had a long way to fall.

D In 1885, John Starley launched the Rover Safety Bicycle, the first model to adopt what we now think of as the traditional design. The bicycle industry was unimpressed, as it had a chain-driven rear wheel, which added weight, and a low seat, which made male riders look a bit ridiculous. But it turned out to be faster than a penny farthing because it was more aerodynamic. More importantly, the Rover could be ridden in a skirt. It was more expensive than a penny farthing, but its practicality was just what the public wanted. Soon there were half a million bicycles in the UK. Between 1890 and 1900, the bicycle was refined until the basic design became very similar to the featherweights that modern champions ride in the Tour de France. Lightweight steel tubing, the diamond-shaped frame, gears and pneumatic tyres with separate inner tubes all became common. Top speeds of 25 mph could now be reached. At last the cyclist could outrun a galloping horse.

Writing (1 hour 20 minutes)

PART 1

You must *answer this question. Write your answer in 140–190 words in an appropriate style.*

1   In your English class you have been talking about The News on television and in other media.
Now, your English teacher has asked you to write an essay.
Write an essay using all the notes and give reasons for your point of view.

> What kind of news in the media has the most influence on people?
>
>
> **Notes**
> Write about:
> 1. politics
> 2. crime
> 3. _____ (your own idea)

PART 2

Write an answer to one of the questions 2–4 in this part. Write your answer in 140–190 words in an appropriate style.

2   You recently saw this notice in an international magazine.

> ### LOCAL REPORTERS WANTED!
> We're looking for people to send us reports on what has been happening in their village, city or region over the past year. You can tell us about important events, ordinary day-to-day life, people in general or specific individuals.
>
> We'll publish some of the reports in a special section.

Write your **report**.

3   You have seen the following announcement on an international student website.

> ### ARE YOU A MEMBER OF A CLUB? TELL US ABOUT IT.
> Write an article about a club that you are a member of.
> Why do you like being a member of it?
> We'll put the best articles in a special section on the website.

Write your **article**.

4   You have seen this announcement in an English-language magazine.

> ### FANCY YOURSELF AS AN INTERVIEWER?
> Is there someone that you'd like to interview? It doesn't have to be a living person. Write and tell us who you'd like to interview if you had the chance. Why would you like to interview that person? What would you ask?
>
> We'll publish the best letters in the next issue.

Write your **letter**.

Listening (40 minutes)

PART 1

You will hear people talking in eight different situations. For questions 1–8, choose the best answer (A, B or C).

1 You hear part of an interview with a sportsman.
What does he say about playing for the national team?

    A He doesn't think it will happen soon.

    B It isn't his main concern at the moment.   **1**

    C The possibility of it happening has put him under pressure.

2 You hear the introduction to a radio programme.
What is the speaker doing?

    A contrasting weather forecasting in the past and the present

    B explaining why weather forecasting has become more accurate   **2**

    C joking about how people used to forecast the weather

3 You hear a man talking about reading aloud to children.
What opinion does he express?

    A Short stories are better than longer books.

    B The choice of book may not be important.   **3**

    C It's hard to know what will make children laugh.

4 You hear someone talking about work.
What is his situation?

    A He has just left a job.

    B He is thinking of leaving his job.   **4**

    C He has just started a new job.

5 You hear someone talking about his childhood.
   What does he mention?

   A a habit he regards as strange

   B regret about some of his behaviour   5

   C how much he has changed

TEST 2

6 You hear someone talking about something that happened at a party.
   How did the speaker feel?

   A upset

   B amused   6

   C frightened

7 You hear part of a talk about blues music.
   What is the speaker talking about?

   A why it originated in a certain area

   B how popular it was in the past compared with today   7

   C its importance in the history of popular music

8 You hear someone on the radio talking about a website for consumers.
   What is the speaker's purpose?

   A to encourage consumers to make complaints

   B to inform consumers about a source of information   8

   C to describe common problems for consumers

PART 2

You will hear a radio reporter talking about indoor skydiving. For questions 9–18, complete the sentences with a word or short phrase.

INDOOR SKYDIVING

The fans in the tunnel are normally used for putting air into **9** _____ .

It has been said that the machine works like a huge **10** _____ .

The walls in the tunnel are made of **11** _____ .

The only parts of the body that can get hurt in the tunnel are the

12 _____ and _____ .

You have to be **13** _____ years old to use the tunnel.

You have to wear **14** _____ when you use the tunnel.

Beginners have two **15** _____ lessons in the tunnel with an

instructor.

During lessons, you get into a position as if you have a **16** _____

in your hands.

The person who created the wind tunnel refers to it as a **17** '_____'.

Indoor skydiving has become a sport called **18** _____ .

You will hear five different people talking about the reasons why they became very successful. For questions 19–23, choose from the list (A–H) the reason each person gives for their success. Use the letters only once. There are three extra letters which you do not need to use.

A   natural ability

	Speaker 1	19

B   lessons learnt from making mistakes

	Speaker 2	20

C   encouragement from others

	Speaker 3	21

D   careful planning

	Speaker 4	22

E   constant good luck

	Speaker 5	23

F   determination to improve

G   good advice from others

H   lack of competition

PART 4

You will hear part of a radio interview with a woman called Tania Wade about taking up running as a regular activity. For questions 24–30, choose the best answer (A, B or C).

24 Tania says that when she was younger,
   A she envied people who did a lot of physical activity.
   B she knew that she ought to take up some kind of physical activity.
   C she hated the idea of doing any kind of physical activity.

   `24`

25 Tania says that if people take up running,
   A she can guarantee that there will be certain benefits.
   B they will wonder why they didn't do it before.
   C it will become a long-term interest for them.

   `25`

26 Tania says that, in comparison with other activities and sports, running is
   A more enjoyable.
   B more convenient.
   C more beneficial.

   `26`

27 What does Tania say about people who feel that they can't take up running?
   A They should talk to people who do run.
   B They may be right.
   C They know that their attitude is wrong.

   `27`

28 Tania warns people who take up running not to
   A be competitive.
   B give up as soon as there is a problem.
   C ignore pain.

   `28`

29 What advice does Tania give about running technique?
   A Change the position of your arms from time to time.
   B Think of your arms as if they were parts of an engine.
   C Pay more attention to your arms than any other part of your body.

   `29`

30 What does Tania say about breathing while running?
   A Some bad advice is sometimes given about it.
   B It takes some time to develop the best technique for it.
   C There isn't a correct or incorrect way of doing it.

   `30`

Speaking (14 minutes)

PART 1 (2 minutes)

Family and friends

- Describe briefly the members of your family.
- What kind of things do you talk about with your friends?
- What influence have your family and friends had on you?
- What interests do your family and friends have?

Money and possessions

- What would you buy if you suddenly had a lot of money? ..... (Why?)
- Do you want to be richer than you are now? ..... (Why? / Why not?)
- What do people of your age generally want to buy? ..... (Why?)
- What are your favourite possessions? ..... (Why?)

Food and cooking

- What do you usually have for breakfast?
- What is your favourite evening meal?
- What dish(es) are you good at cooking?
- Do you have a healthy diet?

PART 2 (4 minutes)

1 Films
2 Cooking

Candidate A	Look at the two photographs 1A and 1B on page 44. They show adverts for films.
	Compare the photographs and say what the characteristics of each kind of film are.
	Candidate A talks on his / her own for about 1 minute.
Candidate B	Which of the films would you prefer to see, and why?
	Candidate B talks on his / her own for about 30 seconds.
Candidate B	Look at the two photographs 2A and 2B on page 44. They show people cooking meals.
	Compare the photographs and say what you think the situation is in each photograph.
	Candidate B talks on his / her own for about 1 minute.
Candidate A	Which of the people cooking would you prefer to be, and why?
	Candidate A talks on his / her own for about 30 seconds.

■ What are the characteristics of each kind of film?

1A

1B

■ What do you think the situation is?

2A

2B

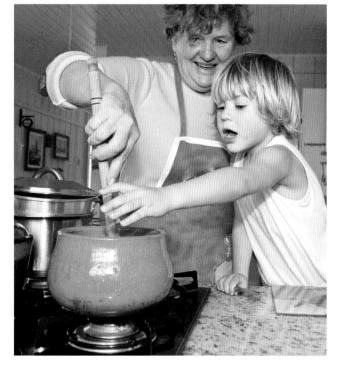

PARTS 3 AND 4 (8 minutes)

'Special day' prize

PART 3 (4 minutes)

Imagine that you are organizing a competition at the place where you work or study. The prize for the winner is going to be a special day and you have to choose what kind of special day the prize will be. Look at the special days offered by a company in their brochure.

First, talk to each other about how attractive each of the possible prizes would be.

Then decide which one should be the prize.

Candidates A and B discuss this together for about 3 minutes.

PART 4 (4 minutes)

- Which of the special days would you like to experience personally? ..... (Why?)
- Which of the special days would you definitely not want to take part in? ...... (Why?)
- What dangerous sports are popular in your country?
- What makes people want to take part in dangerous sports?
- Why do people like going to theme parks? Which ones are good and which ones are not, in your opinion?
- Some people say that young people don't have a wide range of interests. Do you agree?

Reading and Use of English (1 hour 15 minutes)

For questions 1–8, read the text below and decide which answer (A, B, C or D) best fits each gap. There is an example at the beginning (0).

Mark your answers **on the separate answer sheet.**

Example:

0 A convince   **B** guess   **C** believe   **D** value

0	A	B	C	D

Neighbours influence buying decisions

However objective we **0**_____ ourselves to be, most of us do not judge a product solely on its merits, considering quality, value and style before making a decision. **1**_____ , we are easily influenced by the people around us. There is nothing **2**_____ with this. It is probably a smarter way to make decisions than **3**_____ on only our own opinions.

Research in Finland recently found overwhelming evidence that neighbours have a big influence on buying decisions. When one of a person's ten nearest neighbours bought a car, the **4**_____ that that person would buy a car of the same brand during the next week and a half **5**_____ by 86 per cent. The researchers argued that it was not just a **6**_____ of envy. Used cars seemed to attract neighbours even more than new cars. This suggested that people were not trying to **7**_____ up with their neighbours, they were keen to learn from them. Since used cars are less reliable, a recommendation of one can **8**_____ influence a buying decision.

1	**A** What's more	**B** Instead	**C** Unlike	**D** In place
2	**A** wrong	**B** silly	**C** bad	**D** daft
3	**A** basing	**B** trusting	**C** supposing	**D** relying
4	**A** chances	**B** potential	**C** possibilities	**D** forecast
5	**A** boosted	**B** rose	**C** enlarged	**D** lifted
6	**A** thing	**B** point	**C** matter	**D** fact
7	**A** keep	**B** stay	**C** hold	**D** follow
8	**A** fiercely	**B** strongly	**C** firmly	**D** intensely

For questions 9–16, read the text below and think of the word which best fits each gap. Use only **one** *word in each gap. There is an example at the beginning (0).*

Write your answers **IN CAPITAL LETTERS on the separate answer sheet.**

Example:

| 0 | S | O | M | E | T | H | I | N | G | | | |

Learning a musical instrument

Learning to play an instrument is **0** _____ that can give a lot of pleasure. It's also an achievement and a skill **9** _____ stays with you for life. Music has a part to play in everyone's life, and has been described **10** _____ a 'primary language'.

    A lot of adults regret not **11** _____ learnt to play an instrument when they were younger. But it is never **12** _____ late to learn! And the advantages of learning an instrument are far greater than just the pleasure of producing a marvellous sound. When you've progressed far **13** _____, there are lots of amateur groups which you can join **14** _____ you want to be part of a larger group. Once you've reached a good enough standard to join a band or orchestra, you add the team skills like **15** _____ you get from playing sport. There's also a great social side to playing with others, as **16** _____ as the chance to travel through touring.

TEST 3

PART 3

For questions 17–24, read the text below. Use the word given in capitals at the end of some of the lines to form a word that fits in the gap in the same line. There is an example at the beginning (0).

Write your answers IN CAPITAL LETTERS on the separate answer sheet.

Example:

0	F	R	I	E	N	D	L	Y				

THE COUPLES WITH IDENTICAL LIVES

When Frank and Vera Jackson met a **0**_____ couple on holiday   FRIEND

in Spain also called Frank and Vera (but with a different

surname: Bentley), at first they must have laughed at the **17**_____ .   COINCIDE

But when they got into **18**_____ with their namesakes, they made   CONVERSE

some surprising **19**_____ and realized that they had much more in   DISCOVER

common.

    Both couples had had their **20**_____ on the same date in the   WED

same year and at the same time. Both couples each had two daughters, with

dates of **21**_____ in the same years, and six grandchildren. Mr Jackson   BORN

worked in the car industry in Oxford; Mr Bentley had done **22**_____   EXACT

the same job but in Dagenham. Their wives, who had both worked for the

same bank, had both lost their **23**_____ rings and were wearing   ENGAGE

identical gold watches. 'I'm sure people everywhere lead identical

lives,' said Mr Jackson, 'but to meet our doubles was **24**_____ .'   BELIEVE

PART 4

For questions 25–30, complete the second sentence so that it has a similar meaning to the first sentence, using the word given. Do not change the word given. *You must use between two and five words, including the word given. Here is an example (0).*

Example:

0   Making new friends was easy for her.

DIFFICULT

She didn't _____ new friends.

The gap can be filled with the words 'find it difficult to make', so you write:

0	FIND IT DIFFICULT TO MAKE

Write only *the missing words* IN CAPITAL LETTERS on the separate answer sheet.

---

25   Her behaviour tends to be bad when she is under pressure.

TENDENCY

She _____ badly when she is under pressure.

26   My brother earns half of what I earn.

TWICE

I earn _____ my brother.

27   I got angry because of the assistant's attitude.

MADE

The assistant's attitude _____ temper.

28   He plays so skilfully that nobody can beat him.

MUCH

He plays with _____ that nobody can beat him.

29   They were late because they got stuck in traffic.

RESULT

They were late _____ stuck in traffic.

30   Yesterday I met one of my friends by chance in the supermarket.

RAN

Yesterday I _____ mine in the supermarket.

PART 5

You are going to read a newspaper article about careers advice. For questions 31–36, choose the answer (A, B, C or D) which you think fits best according to the text.

Mark your answers on the separate answer sheet.

Finding the career that fits your personality

'If you've finished your exams and have absolutely no idea what to do next, you're not alone,' says Sheridan Hughes, an occupational psychologist at Career Analysts, a career counselling service. 'At 18, it can be very difficult to know what you want to do because you don't really know what you're interested in.' Careers guidance, adds Alexis Hallam, one of her colleagues, is generally poor and 'people can end up in the wrong job and stay there for years because they're good at something without actually enjoying it.'

To discover what people are good at, and more fundamentally, what they will enjoy doing, Career Analysts give their clients a battery of personality profile questionnaires and psychometric tests. An in-depth interview follows, in which the test results are discussed and different career paths and options are explored with the aid of an occupational psychologist. Career Analysts offers guidance to everyone, from teenagers to retirees looking for a new focus in life. The service sounded just what I needed. Dividing my time as I do between teaching and freelance journalism, I definitely need advice about consolidating my career. Being too ancient for Career Analysts' student career option guidance and not, unfortunately, at the executive level yet, I opted for the career management package.

This is aimed at people who are established in their jobs and who either want a change or some advice about planning the next step in their careers.

Having filled in a multitude of personality indicator questionnaires at home, I then spent a rather gruelling morning being aptitude-tested at Career Analysts' offices. The tests consisted of logical reasoning followed by verbal, mechanical and spatial aptitude papers. Logical reasoning required me to pick out the next shape in a sequence of triangles, squares and oblongs. I tried my best but knew that it was really a lost cause. I fared rather better when it came to verbal aptitude - finding the odd one out in a series of words couldn't be simpler. My complacency was short-lived, however, when I was confronted with images of levers and pulleys for the mechanical aptitude papers. My mind went blank. I had no idea what would happen to wheel X when string Y was pulled.

Having completed my personality and aptitude tests, I sat down with Sheridan Hughes, who asked me fairly searching personal and professional questions. What do my parents and siblings do for a living? Why had I chosen to do an English degree? 'I need to get a picture of you as a person and how you've come to be who you are,' she explained. 'What we do works

because it's a mixture of science and counselling. We use objective psychometric measures to discover our clients' natural strengths and abilities and then we talk to them about what they want from life.'

There were no real surprises in my own test results, nor in the interview that followed it. 'We're interested in patterns,' Mrs Hughes explained, 'and the pattern for you is strongly verbal and communicative.' This was putting it rather kindly. I had come out as average on the verbal skills test and below average in logic, numerical, perceptual and mechanical reasoning. My spatial visualization was so bad it was almost off the scale. 'A career in cartography, navigation, tiling or architecture would not be playing to your strengths,' she said delicately.

Mrs Hughes encouraged me to expand the writing side of my career and gave me straightforward, practical suggestions as to how I could go about it. 'Widen the scope of your articles,' she said. 'You could develop an interest in medical and psychological fields.' These latter, she said, would sit comfortably with an interest in human behaviour indicated on my personality-profiling questionnaires. She suggested that I consider writing e-learning content for on-line courses, an avenue that would never have occurred to me.

31 Which of the following is mentioned in the first paragraph?

    A people underestimating their own abilities

    B people accepting inappropriate advice

    C people being unwilling to take risks

    D people constantly changing their minds

31

32 What does the writer say about Career Analysts in the second paragraph?

    A It is about to offer a service for people at executive level.

    B The range of services it offers is unique.

    C She was initially doubtful that it could be useful to her.

    D Only one of its services was relevant to her.

32

33 What happened when the writer took the aptitude tests?

    A She found two of the papers extremely difficult.

    B She put in very little effort on any of them.

    C She didn't understand what she was required to do on one of them.

    D The papers were not what she had been expecting.

33

34 Some of the questions Sheridan Hughes asked concerned the writer's

    A opinions of the tests and questionnaires.

    B relationships with family members.

    C main regrets.

    D progress through life.

34

35 The writer felt that during the interview, Mrs Hughes

    A was keen not to upset her concerning her test results.

    B seemed surprised at how badly she had done in the tests.

    C was being honest about her strengths and weaknesses.

    D preferred to avoid talking about her test results.

35

36 The advice Mrs Hughes gave to the writer included the suggestion that she should

    A think about taking a course on writing.

    B concentrate only on writing and not on any other kind of work.

    C increase the number of subjects she writes about.

    D do something she had previously considered unappealing.

36

PART 6

You are going to read an article about martial arts. Six sentences have been removed from the article. Choose from the sentences A–G the one which fits each gap (37–42). There is one extra sentence which you do not need to use.

Mark your answers on the separate answer sheet.

Martial Arts Classes

Learn an effective fighting and self-defence system

Tony Chang is a martial artist who has served a long apprenticeship in both the internal and external arts. He is respected worldwide as a martial arts instructor in kenpo, t'ai chi ch'uan and chi kung and runs several of his own clubs in Manchester. He also has several training videos and DVDs to his credit. In fact, he was one of the pioneers of teaching the Martial Arts Techniques series on the worldwide web. **37** _____

Tony is now in the process of producing what he considers to be the 'ultimate street survival' DVD, combining fighting and self-defence with energy (chi) development and enhancement. A few years ago, he was inducted into the Martial Arts Hall of Fame for integrating his internal martial arts knowledge with the fast-paced external striking style that kenpo is noted for, and developing kenpo taiji. **38** _____

It is not based purely on physical strength. **39** _____ As Tony explains, 'It is 50 per cent physical and 50 per cent in the mind. It is a scientific fact that we have three brains inside our head. As well as the intellectual brain which forms 90 per cent of our overall brain, five per cent is the artistic brain which is responsible for subconscious body movement and five per cent constitutes the reptilian brain, which is purely reflex. This is the same brain as that of all reptiles, such as snakes and crocodiles – this is our survival brain.'

40 _____ That is because they use the logical, intellectual brain to teach logical pre-arranged techniques. However, fighting is totally illogical and we cannot apply logic to an illogical situation, so our response to an attack must be reflex. Students achieve this in kenpo taiji by learning how to access their reptilian brain. Tony says there is no time to think in a fight situation. 'If you stop to think, you'll get hit,' he explains.

Tony is running beginners' classes in kenpo taiji. **41** _____ These include how to adopt certain body postures which encourage energy to flow from an energy storage centre known as the *dan tien* up to the brain stem. Students are then in reptile brain mode, ready to defend themselves against any attacker. And they learn training methods designed by the ancient Chinese masters to programme this part of the brain subconsciously with correct fighting principles.

As well as being an effective fighting and self-defence system, kenpo taiji teaches students to develop and intensify the flow of their own internal energy (chi) by training in chi kung and traditional t'ai chi ch'uan, enabling them to achieve perfect health. **42** _____ And in addition to that, during the classes some of the greatest martial arts secrets are revealed by Tony.

A If that were the case, the stronger, bigger person would always win.

B As a result of such experiences, more and more people are taking it up.

C This is one of the most formidable street survival, fighting and self-defence systems ever invented.

D Students attending these are taught several training methods.

E If you take it up, you will learn how to get into this condition and you will be able to defend yourself whatever your size, age or gender.

F Many others have now followed his lead.

G Most martial arts are not street effective.

Writing (1 hour 20 minutes)

You must *answer this question. Write your answer in 140–190 words in an appropriate style.*

1   In your English class you have been talking about the importance of sport in people's lives.
    Now, your English teacher has asked you to write an essay.
    Write an essay using all the notes and give reasons for your point of view.

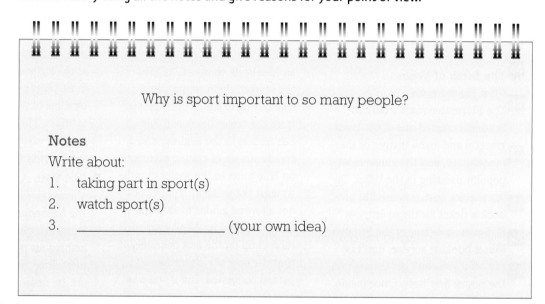

Why is sport important to so many people?

Notes
Write about:

1.   taking part in sport(s)
2.   watch sport(s)
3.   _____ (your own idea)

PART 2

Write an answer to one of the questions 2–4 in this part. Write your answer in 140–190 words in an appropriate style.

---

2   Your college recently staged its annual show, in which students at the college perform. You have been asked to write a review of the show for the college website.

   Write your review.

3   You have seen this announcement in an international magazine.

MY FAVOURITE HOBBY

What's your passion when you're not working or studying? Tell us all about it and why you like it. What does it involve? What made you take it up and how much of your time do you spend on it?

We'll publish the best articles in a special section next month.

   Write your article.

4   You recently saw this notice in an international magazine.

WHAT ARE THE LATEST FASHIONS WHERE YOU ARE?

We're looking for people to send us reports on the latest fashions among young people in the places where they live. You can tell us about fashions in music, in clothes, in what people buy, in behaviour or anything else you want to describe. And give your opinions on these fashions too. We'll publish some of the reports so that our readers can compare fashions in different places.

   Write your report.

Listening (40 minutes)

PART 1

You will hear people talking in eight different situations. For questions 1–8, choose the best answer, (A, B or C).

1   You hear part of an interview with a pop singer.
    How does she feel about what happened?

    A   embarrassed by her mistake

    B   angry with her tour manager   1

    C   confused about what happened

2   You hear part of a radio programme for young people.
    What advice does the speaker give?

    A   Try to discuss the matter with your friends.

    B   Pay no attention to the people who laugh at you.   2

    C   Encourage other people to be like you.

3   You hear a radio presenter talking about a book.
    What does the presenter say about the book?

    A   Some of the writers have already had their work published.

    B   It contains work that was entered for a competition.   3

    C   It is very well organized.

4   You hear someone talking on the phone.
    What is the speaker's purpose?

    A   to resolve a disagreement

    B   to make a threat   4

    C   to apologize for previous behaviour

5   You hear someone talking to an assistant at a box office.
    What is the situation?

    A   The man has lost his tickets.

    B   The man was sent the wrong tickets.   `[ ] 5`

    C   The man wants to return the tickets.

6   You hear someone talking about her personality.
    What is the speaker doing?

    A   admitting something

    B   explaining something   `[ ] 6`

    C   promising something

7   You hear two people talking.
    What is the relationship between them?

    A   They are members of the same club.

    B   They live in the same building.   `[ ] 7`

    C   They are studying on the same course.

8   You hear a local radio presenter talking about a competition.
    Which of the following is true of the competition?

    A   The first part does not involve any cooking.

    B   The second part involves ten people cooking on their own.   `[ ] 8`

    C   The final part takes place at a different restaurant.

You will hear someone introducing a conference for the organizers of music festivals.
For questions 9–18, complete the sentences with a word or short phrase.

CONFERENCE FOR MUSIC FESTIVAL ORGANIZERS

First session

The session will cover disagreements that can happen between festival organizers and

9 _____ .

An expert will give advice on what a **10** _____ should contain.

The session will deal with the issue of **11** _____ at festivals, which affect people's opinions of them.

The session will also focus on how **12** _____ can affect the planning of a festival.

Second session

The session will consider what **13** _____ do in connection with the entertainment provided.

Participants will discuss whether it is a good idea to have competitions that involve a system of

14 _____ .

Third session

The session will focus on how to attract **15** _____ for a festival.

A professional in the area of **16** _____ will address the conference.

Last session

The main topic of the session is ways of **17** _____ festivals.

The practice of having special offers on **18** _____ will also be discussed.

You will hear five different people talking about what they discovered when they read autobiographies by famous people. For questions 19–23, choose from the list (A–H) what each person says that they discovered. Use the letters only once. There are three extra letters which you do not need to use.

A   He had a terrible life before becoming famous.

Speaker 1   **19**

B   He is a nicer person than he appears to be.

Speaker 2   **20**

C   He is exactly the same in private as he is in public.

Speaker 3   **21**

D   He never intended to become so famous.

Speaker 4   **22**

E   He would have preferred a different career.

Speaker 5   **23**

F   He was very unkind to other people after he became famous.

G   He gets very upset by criticsm.

H   He feels that he is a very important person.

PART 2

- Why do you think the person is taking the photograph?

1A

1B

- What is the situation in each photograph?

2A

2B

Planning a local event

PART 3 (4 minutes)

Imagine that a committee is going to organize a one-day event to be enjoyed by people of all ages in the place where you live. Look at the ideas for possible events.

First, talk to each other about why each of these events might be popular.
Then decide which event would be the best one to have.

Candidates A and B discuss this together for about 3 minutes.

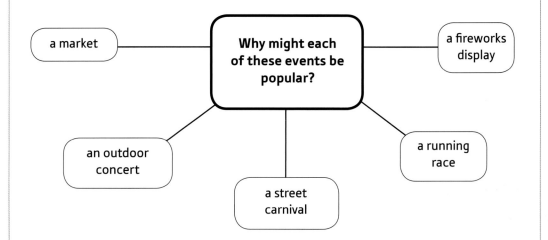

a market

Why might each of these events be popular?

a fireworks display

an outdoor concert

a street carnival

a running race

PART 4 (4 minutes)

- What kind of local events take place where you come from? Do young people take part in or attend them?
- Would you like to organize an event like this? ..... (Why? / Why not?)
- What's the best event you've ever attended? Why was it so good?
- What's the worst event you've ever attended? Why was it so bad?
- Do you think that local life is changing where you come from? ..... (Why / Why not?)
- Some people think that in the modern world, local communities are not as important as they used to be. Do you agree?

TEST 3

Reading and Use of English (1 hour 15 minutes)

PART 1

For questions 1–8, read the text below and decide which answer (A, B, C or D) best fits each gap. There is an example at the beginning (0).

Mark your answers on the separate answer sheet.

Example:

0 **A** notice   **B** attention   **C** regard   **D** interest

0	A	B	C	D

She studies while he plays: true of children and chimps

Little girls watch and learn; little boys don't pay **0**_____ and play around. At least, this seems to be the **1**_____ with chimpanzees, according to new research.

Chimpanzees in the wild **2**_____ to snack on termites, and youngsters learn to fish for them by poking long sticks and other **3**_____ tools into the mounds that large groups of termites build. Researchers found that **4**_____ average female chimps in the Gombe National Park in Tanzania learnt how to do termite fishing at the age of 31 months, more than two years earlier than the males.

The females seem to learn by watching their mothers. Researcher Dr. Elisabeth V. Lonsdorf said that it is **5**_____ to find that, when a young male and female are near a mound, 'she's really focusing on termite fishing and he's spinning himself round **6**_____ circles.' The behaviour of both sexes may seem **7**_____ to many parents, Dr. Lonsdorf said, adding, 'The sex differences we found in the chimps are **8**_____ to some of the findings from human child development research.'

1 **A** case   **B** matter   **C** fact   **D** event
2 **A** delight   **B** enjoy   **C** like   **D** fancy
3 **A** relative   **B** connected   **C** close   **D** similar
4 **A** on   **B** by   **C** at   **D** for
5 **A** ordinary   **B** regular   **C** typical   **D** frequent
6 **A** with   **B** in   **C** to   **D** through
7 **A** acquainted **B** familiar   **C** recognized **D** known
8 **A** corresponding **B** alike   **C** identical   **D** matching

For questions 9–16, read the text below and think of the word which best fits each gap. Use only **one** word in each gap. There is an example at the beginning (0).

Write your answers IN CAPITAL LETTERS on the separate answer sheet.

Example:

| 0 | A | T | | | | | | | | | | | | |

NATIONAL VEGETARIAN WEEK

Around 5% of British households now have **0**_____ least one family member who is vegetarian, **9**_____ means that in the region of 3 million British people are vegetarians. Vegetarians do not eat meat, fish or poultry. Among the many reasons **10**_____ being a vegetarian are health, compassion for animals, and religious beliefs.

Statistically, if you choose **11**_____ vegetarian diet, you are choosing an option which should boost your chances of living a long and healthy life. But why? The reason **12**_____ that a good vegetarian diet contains more carbohydrate, more vitamin C and more fibre **13**_____ one where a high proportion of the calories come from meat.

There is documentary evidence of a Vegetarian Day **14**_____ held in Britain as early as 1936, but National Vegetarian Week **15**_____ we know it today has its roots in the National Vegetarian Day held by the Vegetarian Society in October 1991. It proved **16**_____ successful that they extended it to a whole week.

TEST 4

PART 3

For questions 17–24, read the text below. Use the word given in capitals at the end of some of the lines to form a word that fits in the gap in the same line. There is an example at the beginning (0).

Write your answers IN CAPITAL LETTERS on the separate answer sheet.

Example:

| 0 | L | E | A | D | I | N | G | | | | | | |

WHEN BOSSES MAKE SPEECHES

For business managers, public speaking is part of the job. A survey of

100 **0** _____ companies found that chief executives received on   **LEAD**

average 175 **17** _____ a year to speak at conferences. Some   **INVITE**

executives love public speaking but some have an enormous

18 _____ for it.   **LIKE**

   There are plenty of experts giving **19** _____ to them on how to   **ADVISE**

interest **20** _____ . According to Carmine Gallo, author of a book   **LISTEN**

on public speaking, it is essential to avoid giving too much information

and to keep the audience's **21** _____ . He points to the example of   **ATTEND**

one executive whose **22** _____ involves walking off the stage   **TECHNICAL**

and into the audience, where he asks a question or rests a hand

on a person's shoulder in the style of a television talk-show host.

Speaking without notes, he **23** _____ that he maintains   **SURE**

constant eye contact with his audience.

   And then there was a **24** _____ public speaker who would   **LEGEND**

gather his ideas before a speech, jotting notes on a pad. People would

ask for a copy of the speech after he had spoken but no such thing existed.

PART 4

For questions 25–30, complete the second sentence so that it has a similar meaning to the first sentence, using the word given. Do not change the word given. You must use between two and five words, including the word given. Here is an example (0).

Example:

0   Making new friends was easy for her.

DIFFICULT

She didn't _____ new friends.

The gap can be filled with the words 'find it difficult to make', so you write:

0	FIND IT DIFFICULT TO MAKE

Write only *the missing words* IN CAPITAL LETTERS on the separate answer sheet.

---

25   It says here that we should we reply to this invitation.

SUPPOSED

It says here that _____ to this invitation.

26   I haven't got my wallet – it must be at home.

LEFT

I haven't got my wallet – I _____ at home.

27   Is it likely that this invention will become popular with the public?

CATCH

Is this invention likely _____ with the public?

28   There are a minimum of seven classes a week during the course.

LEAST

The course consists _____ seven classes a week.

29   My sister can't drive so she hasn't got her own car.

KNOW

My sister _____ drive so she hasn't got her own car.

30   I wrote down his email address on a piece of paper.

NOTE

I _____ his email address on a piece of paper.

You are going to read a newspaper article about holidays. For questions 31–36, choose the answer (A, B, C or D) which you think fits best according to the text.

Mark your answers on the separate answer sheet.

Why I've taken a break from holidays

It is now close to four years since I last took a holiday. This is because I have come to the conclusion, over the course of my adult life, that I am not very good at it. You might think this sounds like saying you're not very good at drinking tea or listening to music. What could possibly be difficult about the natural act of putting your working life on hold for a couple of weeks and going somewhere warm to do nothing?

To be honest, I'm a little baffled myself. I was a model holidaymaker as a kid: every July, I would arrive at an Italian campsite with my parents and, within a couple of days, my skin would have turned an olive colour and I would blend into my surroundings so totally that I would often find myself being mistakenly told to join a party of local schoolchildren. The problems started during my early twenties: a stolen tent and wallet at the Glastonbury Festival in 1995; a lightning strike and sudden drop in altitude on a flight over the Channel in 1997; an ill-fated experiment in 'luxury inter-railing' in 1998 that lasted just four days and ended with the French police mistaking me for a drug smuggler.

But even if I manage to go away without being mugged or getting food poisoning, I now find that I can't really commit to the experience. A fancy-free trip to the South of France five years ago to 'just kind of hang out on the coast' was ended after just two days, mainly because I had an urge to check my e-mails. Similarly, my honeymoon, a year or so later, was cut short by 48 hours – not because my wife and I weren't enjoying ourselves, but because we were missing our cats.

So what is my problem? On the surface, I'm probably a bit of a homebody. And I just find the pressure of being on holiday too severe: it always feels like having a gun held to my head and being forced to have fun. Somehow, packing a carefully itemised list of possessions and meeting a scheduled flight has none of the excitement of suddenly deciding to take a day off and driving somewhere for the fun of it.

Thankfully, I'm not alone. This summer, most of my friends have decided not to have a break. And a recent survey highlighted the downside of holidays, with the results showing that nearly two thirds of people found that the calming effects of a holiday wore off within 24 hours, as stress levels returned to normal. And this year *The Idler* magazine published its *Book of Awful Holidays*. Here you will find a list of the five most ecologically-damaging vacations it's possible to take, along with 50 horrific holiday experiences voted for on *The Idler* website. Over the last decade, *The Idler* has become well known for promoting the idea of an easy, lazy life. The leisure industry might seem an unlikely target of its criticism, but Dan Kiernan, the book's editor, says that he was flooded with entries from readers for his list of Awful Holidays.

'What interests me is what the concept of a "holiday" says about the rest of our lives,' he explains. For me, the point of living is to have a life you enjoy for 52 weeks a year.' **He has a point.** The more I like my life and the better I structure it, the less I want to go away. Maybe I'm weird for not liking holidays, but I just feel my leisure time is too valuable to waste on them.

31 What does the writer suggest about the fact that he has not taken a holiday for four years?

    A Some people may find the reason surprising.

    B He often has to explain the reason to other people.

    C There have been times when he has regretted it.

    D It is not something he has thought about before.

`31`

32 What is the writer describing in the second paragraph?

    A events that explain why he has never really liked holidays

    B events that he regards as not typical of most people's experiences

    C events that illustrate his contrasting experiences of holidays

    D events that he did not consider particularly serious when they happened

`32`

33 The events the writer describes in the third paragraph illustrate

    A how hard he has tried to enjoy holidays.

    B how badly he behaves when he is on holiday.

    C his fear that something bad will happen when he is on holiday.

    D his lack of enthusiasm for being on holiday.

`33`

34 The writer says in the fourth paragraph that the main thing he dislikes about holidays is that

    A they are often organized in order to please other people.

    B they are far less enjoyable than breaks that have not been planned in advance.

    C he tends to be made responsible for too much of the organization of them.

    D he feels embarrassed when other people are having fun but he isn't.

`34`

35 The writer says that a recent survey shows that a lot of people

    A pretend to enjoy their holidays.

    B fail to relax while they are on holiday.

    C feel that the benefits of going on holiday are limited.

    D have made the same decision as the writer and most of his friends.

`35`

36 The writer says that the book published by *The Idler* magazine

    A illustrates a point that the magazine has often made.

    B proved more popular than he would have expected.

    C focuses entirely on bad personal experiences of holidays.

    D indicates that his dislike of holidays is widely shared.

`36`

TEST 4

You are going to read an article about maps showing the homes of film stars. Six sentences have been removed from the article. Choose from the sentences A–G the one which fits each gap (37–42). There is one extra sentence which you do not need to use.

Mark your answers on the separate answer sheet.

Maps of the stars

Ever since the 1910s, when film-makers like Cecil B. DeMille first set up shop in Hollywood, mapmakers, the explorers of the city's social terrain, have been compiling that only-in-Los Angeles fixture, maps showing the locations of the fabulous homes of the stars. Collectively, they form an unofficial version of the Oscars, reflecting who's in and who's out in the film world. 'Each one looks different,' says Linda Welton, whose grandfather and mother pioneered these maps. **37** _____ Former icons vanish from them, new ones appear on them, and some of the truly greats are permanent fixtures on them.

In 1933, noticing the steady stream of tourists drifting westward to follow the stars from Hollywood to Beverly Hills, the nearby district where most of the stars went to live, Ms Welton's grandfather, Wesley G Lake, obtained a copyright for his *Guide to Starland Estates and Mansions*. **38** _____ For 40 years Ms Welton's mother, Vivienne E Welton, sold maps just down the road from Gary Cooper's place at 200 Baroda*. The asterisk indicates that it was the actor's final home, as opposed to a plus sign (denoting a former home) or a zero (for no view from the street).

'My grandfather asked Mom to talk to the gardeners to find out where the stars lived,' Ms Welton recalls. 'She'd say: "Oh, this is a beautiful garden. Who lives here?" Who would suspect a little girl?' Ms Welton and her crew now sell about 10,000 maps a year from a folding chair parked curbside six days a week. **39** _____

The evolution of the maps mirrors both the Hollywood publicity machine and real estate and tourism development. **40** _____ The first celebrity home, according to Marc Wanamaker, a historian and a founder of the Westwood and Beverly Hills Historical Societies, belonged to the artist Paul de Longpre. He had a luxuriously-landscaped house at Cahuenga Avenue and Hollywood and real estate

agents would take prospective clients past it on tours.

Although it is not known for certain who published the first map, by the mid-1920s all sorts of people were producing them. **41** _____

One of the most famous of the early maps was produced to show the location of Pickfair, the sprawling home of the newly married stars Mary Pickford and Douglas Fairbanks Sr, and the homes of some of their star friends. During World War I, they opened their home to serve refreshments to soldiers. As Vivienne Welton once explained in an interview with *Mercator's World*, a map and cartography magazine, 'She urged a few friends to do the same. **42** _____ '

For over 40 years, people have marched toward the corner of Sunset and Baroda with hand-painted yellow signs saying: 'Star Maps, 2 blocks', 'Star Maps, 1 block', 'Star Maps here'. The maps reflect the shifting geography of stardom as celebrities, seeking escape from over-enthusiastic fans, some with ill intentions, have moved out to other locations.

A As they do so, they give advice to the tourists on star safaris through the lime green landscape of Beverly Hills.

B Studios like Paramount published the names and addresses of its stars on theirs, and businesses distributed them as a promotional gimmick.

C Others, however, say that the star maps are still an essential part of Hollywood and the film world.

D Early film stars like Lillian Gish lived in modest, somewhat grubby rooming houses, taking street cars to and from the studio.

E Updated regularly, they are still for sale at the corner of Sunset Boulevard and Baroda Drive.

F And so a map was needed.

G It is the oldest continuously published star map and one of a half-dozen or so maps of varying degrees of accuracy and spelling correctness sold today.

Listening (40 minutes)

<u>PART 1</u>

You will hear people talking in eight different situations. For questions 1–8, choose the best answer, (A, B or C).

___

1 You hear someone talking on a radio programme.
   What is the speaker doing?

   A recommending that listeners make a certain drink

   B explaining why a drink is becoming more popular | 1 |

   C telling listeners about a drink they may not know about

2 You hear someone talking about people who travel a lot when they're young.
   What is his attitude towards these people?

   A He is envious of them for having the opportunity.

   B He feels that they are simply wasting their time. | 2 |

   C He can't understand why they do it.

3 You hear an advertisement for a course.
   What does the speaker say about the course?

   A You need to take a test before being accepted for it.

   B It starts with theory and moves on to practical work. | 3 |

   C It focuses on your effect on the people you will instruct.

4 You hear part of a radio interview.
   Who is being interviewed?

   A a film director

   B an actor | 4 |

   C a screenwriter

5 You hear part of a radio report about car drivers.
What did the survey discover about a lot of drivers?

A They pay no attention to warning lights.

B They don't know what various symbols in a car relate to. 　　　**5**

C They think there are too many warning lights and symbols in cars.

6 You turn on the radio and hear part of a programme.
What type of programme is it?

A a review programme

B a chat show 　　　**6**

C a phone-in

7 You hear part of a radio play.
Where is the scene taking place?

A in a restaurant

B in a car 　　　**7**

C in a house

8 You hear a woman talking about running.
What aspect of running is she talking about?

A her involvement in running over a period of time

B why she finds running so enjoyable 　　　**8**

C the importance of running and training with others

You will hear an announcement about a competition. For questions 9–18, complete the sentences with a word or short phrase.

THE IDEAS COMPETITION

The money given to the winner is not a **9** _____ .

The winner might be **10** _____ with a plan for improving a water supply.

The winner might have an idea about how to help the **11** _____ in the world.

If you enter the competition by phone you must explain your idea in a maximum of **12** _____ .

One of the categories is for people who want to start a business that provides a **13** _____ or _____ that currently doesn't exist.

One of the categories is for people who want to take part in a project that is **14** _____ .

One of the rules is that **15** _____ for the competition are not allowed.

Before you phone, it may be a good idea to prepare a **16** _____ .

To win, you must show that you have a lot of **17** _____ for your idea.

Judges will listen to the ideas presented by **18** _____ people.

You will hear five different people talking about how they felt when they received an award.
For questions 19–23, choose from the list (A–H) how each person felt. Use the letters only
once. There are three extra letters which you do not need to use.

A relieved

Speaker 1   19

B worried

Speaker 2   20

C proud

Speaker 3   21

D exhausted

Speaker 4   22

E embarrassed

Speaker 5   23

F grateful

G confused

H amused

TEST 4

You will hear an interview with someone who has started a magazine for children. For questions 24–30, choose the best answer (A, B or C).

24 When talking about her job as a primary school teacher, Kate emphasizes
   A how much effort the job required.
   B how good she was as a teacher.
   C how difficult the children could be.

[ ] 24

25 Kate decided to start her own magazine for children
   A because both children and parents suggested the idea.
   B when she was working in publishing for children.
   C after considering what was available for children.

[ ] 25

26 What does Kate say about enthusiasm?
   A Children respond positively to it.
   B Children cannot maintain it for long.
   C Children experience it more than adults.

[ ] 26

27 Kate says that she learnt from her research that children
   A don't want to feel that they are being considered inferior.
   B don't like texts that have too much serious content.
   C don't know some words that she had expected them to know.

[ ] 27

28 Kate says that the age range for the magazine
   A may change to some extent in the future.
   B may not be exactly what it is stated to be.
   C has been decided after asking parents.

[ ] 28

29 Kate says that the magazine makes use of the Internet because
   A some children prefer using it to learn about subjects.
   B some subjects cannot be covered fully in the magazine.
   C it is used a great deal in connection with some school work.

[ ] 29

30 Kate says that one of her aims for the magazine is to
   A include subjects that children don't normally read about.
   B create an interest in subjects some children consider boring.
   C encourage children to choose what they want as a career.

[ ] 30

Speaking (14 minutes)

<u>PART 1</u> (2 minutes)

Music

- What's your favourite kind of music? ..... (Why?)
- What kind(s) of music don't you like? ..... (Why?)
- What kinds of music are popular with young people in your country? ..... (Why?)
- Have you ever tried to play a musical instrument? Did you do well?

Technology / Gadgets

- What pieces of technology or electronic gadgets do you own?
- How did you learn how to use pieces of technology or electronic gadgets?
- What do you think are the advantages and disadvantages of new technology for communicating with other people? ..... (Why?)
- Which pieces of technology or electronic gadgets would you like to own? ..... (Why?)

Books and reading

- Do you spend a lot of time reading? ..... (Why? / Why not?)
- What kind of books do you particularly like reading?
- Describe the last book that you read.
- Apart from books, what kind of things do you read?

<u>PART 2</u> (4 minutes)

1 Working life
2 Visiting a city

Candidate A	Look at the two photographs 1A and 1B on page 84. They show people working.
	Compare the photographs and say what the people's working lives are like.
	Candidate A talks on his / her own for about 1 minute.
Candidate B	Which of the situations would you prefer to be in, and why?
	Candidate B talks on his / her own for about 30 seconds.
Candidate B	Look at the two photographs 2A and 2B on page 84. They show visitors to a city.
	Compare the photographs and say what kind of trips the people are on.
	Candidate B talks on his / her own for about 1 minute.
Candidate A	Which of the trips would you prefer to take?
	Candidate A talks on his / her own for about 30 seconds.

TEST 4

■ What are the people's working lives like?

1A

1B

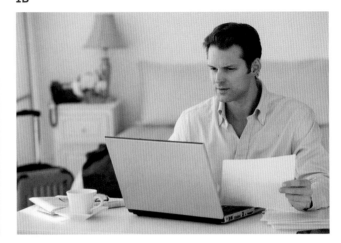

■ What kind of trips are the people on?

2A

2B

A day with a visitor

PART 3 (4 minutes)

Imagine that a friend of yours has a friend from another country staying with him / her. Your friend has to go out for a day next week and has asked you to look after the visitor for a day. Look at the ideas for what you could do with the visitor for that day.

First, talk to each other about which of the activities would be good for the visitor and good for you.

Then decide which two activities to do with the visitor and plan the day.

Candidates A and B discuss this together for about 3 minutes.

walk in the countryside

Which of the activities would be good for the visitor and good for you?

go to a shopping centre

see a film at a cinema

stay at home talking

visit a museum or art gallery

PART 4 (4 minutes)

- If a visitor from another country came to stay with you, what would be the first place you would take that person to? ..... (Why?)
- What place(s) would you certainly not take a visitor to? ..... (Why?)
- Do many overseas visitors come to your country? ..... (Why? / Why not?)
- When you go out with friends, what sort of places do you go to and what do you do there?
- How active are young people in your country? Do they prefer to do things that involve sitting down for long periods?
- What entertainment is available in the place where you live? What other kinds of entertainment do you think should be available?
- Some people say that too much entertainment is available to people and so they are unable to entertain themselves. Do you agree?

TEST 4

Cambridge English: First Practice Test 1

Name ....

READING AND USE OF ENGLISH

PART 1: Mark ONE letter for each question.

1	A B C D		5	A B C D
2	A B C D		6	A B C D
3	A B C D		7	A B C D
4	A B C D		8	A B C D

PART 2: Write your answers clearly IN CAPITAL LETTERS. Write one letter in each box.

9	
10	
11	
12	
13	
14	
15	
16	

PART 3: Write your answers clearly IN CAPITAL LETTERS. Write one letter in each box.

17	
18	
19	
20	
21	
22	
23	
24	

PART 4: Write only the missing words IN CAPITAL LETTERS.

25	
26	
27	
28	
29	
30	

PART 5: Mark ONE letter for each question.

31	A B C D		34	A B C D
32	A B C D		35	A B C D
33	A B C D		36	A B C D

PART 6: Mark ONE letter for each question.

37	A	B	C	D	E	F	G
38	A	B	C	D	E	F	G
39	A	B	C	D	E	F	G

40	A	B	C	D	E	F	G
41	A	B	C	D	E	F	G
42	A	B	C	D	E	F	G

PART 7: Mark ONE letter for each question.

43	A	B	C	D
44	A	B	C	D
45	A	B	C	D
46	A	B	C	D
47	A	B	C	D

48	A	B	C	D
49	A	B	C	D
50	A	B	C	D
51	A	B	C	D
52	A	B	C	D

LISTENING

PART 1: Mark ONE letter for each question.

1	A	B	C
2	A	B	C
3	A	B	C
4	A	B	C

5	A	B	C
6	A	B	C
7	A	B	C
8	A	B	C

PART 2: Write your answers clearly IN CAPITAL LETTERS. Write one letter in each box.

9																	
10																	
11																	
12																	
13																	
14																	
15																	
16																	
17																	
18																	

PART 3: Mark ONE letter for each question.

19	A	B	C	D	E	F	G	H
20	A	B	C	D	E	F	G	H
21	A	B	C	D	E	F	G	H
22	A	B	C	D	E	F	G	H
23	A	B	C	D	E	F	G	H

PART 4: Mark ONE letter for each question.

24	A	B	C
25	A	B	C
26	A	B	C
27	A	B	C

28	A	B	C
29	A	B	C
30	A	B	C

Cambridge English: First   Practice Test 2

Name ....

READING AND USE OF ENGLISH

PART 1: Mark ONE letter for each question.

1	A	B	C	D
2	A	B	C	D
3	A	B	C	D
4	A	B	C	D

5	A	B	C	D
6	A	B	C	D
7	A	B	C	D
8	A	B	C	D

PART 2: Write your answers clearly IN CAPITAL LETTERS. Write one letter in each box.

9																		
10																		
11																		
12																		
13																		
14																		
15																		
16																		

PART 3: Write your answers clearly IN CAPITAL LETTERS. Write one letter in each box.

17																		
18																		
19																		
20																		
21																		
22																		
23																		
24																		

PART 4: Write only the missing words IN CAPITAL LETTERS.

25	
26	
27	
28	
29	
30	

PART 5: Mark ONE letter for each question.

31	A	B	C	D
32	A	B	C	D
33	A	B	C	D

34	A	B	C	D
35	A	B	C	D
36	A	B	C	D

PART 6: Mark ONE letter for each question.

37	A	B	C	D	E	F	G
38	A	B	C	D	E	F	G
39	A	B	C	D	E	F	G

40	A	B	C	D	E	F	G
41	A	B	C	D	E	F	G
42	A	B	C	D	E	F	G

PART 7: Mark ONE letter for each question.

43	A	B	C	D
44	A	B	C	D
45	A	B	C	D
46	A	B	C	D
47	A	B	C	D

48	A	B	C	D
49	A	B	C	D
50	A	B	C	D
51	A	B	C	D
52	A	B	C	D

LISTENING

PART 1: Mark ONE letter for each question.

1	A	B	C
2	A	B	C
3	A	B	C
4	A	B	C

5	A	B	C
6	A	B	C
7	A	B	C
8	A	B	C

PART 2: Write your answers clearly IN CAPITAL LETTERS. Write one letter in each box.

9																		
10																		
11																		
12																		
13																		
14																		
15																		
16																		
17																		
18																		

PART 3: Mark ONE letter for each question.

19	A	B	C	D	E	F	G	H
20	A	B	C	D	E	F	G	H
21	A	B	C	D	E	F	G	H
22	A	B	C	D	E	F	G	H
23	A	B	C	D	E	F	G	H

PART 4: Mark ONE letter for each question.

24	A	B	C
25	A	B	C
26	A	B	C
27	A	B	C

28	A	B	C
29	A	B	C
30	A	B	C

ANSWER SHEET

Cambridge English: First Practice Test 3

Name ....

READING AND USE OF ENGLISH

PART 1: Mark ONE letter for each question.

1	A	B	C	D		5	A	B	C	D
2	A	B	C	D		6	A	B	C	D
3	A	B	C	D		7	A	B	C	D
4	A	B	C	D		8	A	B	C	D

PART 2: Write your answers clearly IN CAPITAL LETTERS. Write one letter in each box.

9																			
10																			
11																			
12																			
13																			
14																			
15																			
16																			

PART 3: Write your answers clearly IN CAPITAL LETTERS. Write one letter in each box.

17																			
18																			
19																			
20																			
21																			
22																			
23																			
24																			

PART 4: Write only the missing words IN CAPITAL LETTERS.

25	
26	
27	
28	
29	
30	

PART 5: Mark ONE letter for each question.

31	A	B	C	D		34	A	B	C	D
32	A	B	C	D		35	A	B	C	D
33	A	B	C	D		36	A	B	C	D

PHOTOCOPIABLE

ANSWER SHEET

PART 6: Mark ONE letter for each question.

37	A	B	C	D	E	F	G
38	A	B	C	D	E	F	G
39	A	B	C	D	E	F	G

40	A	B	C	D	E	F	G
41	A	B	C	D	E	F	G
42	A	B	C	D	E	F	G

PART 7: Mark ONE letter for each question.

43	A	B	C	D
44	A	B	C	D
45	A	B	C	D
46	A	B	C	D
47	A	B	C	D

48	A	B	C	D
49	A	B	C	D
50	A	B	C	D
51	A	B	C	D
52	A	B	C	D

LISTENING

PART 1: Mark ONE letter for each question.

1	A	B	C
2	A	B	C
3	A	B	C
4	A	B	C

5	A	B	C
6	A	B	C
7	A	B	C
8	A	B	C

PART 2: Write your answers clearly IN CAPITAL LETTERS. Write one letter in each box.

9																			
10																			
11																			
12																			
13																			
14																			
15																			
16																			
17																			
18																			

PART 3: Mark ONE letter for each question.

19	A	B	C	D	E	F	G	H
20	A	B	C	D	E	F	G	H
21	A	B	C	D	E	F	G	H
22	A	B	C	D	E	F	G	H
23	A	B	C	D	E	F	G	H

PART 4: Mark ONE letter for each question.

24	A	B	C
25	A	B	C
26	A	B	C
27	A	B	C

28	A	B	C
29	A	B	C
30	A	B	C

Cambridge English: First Practice Test 4

Name ....

ANSWER SHEET

READING AND USE OF ENGLISH

PART 1: Mark ONE letter for each question.

1	A B C D
2	A B C D
3	A B C D
4	A B C D

5	A B C D
6	A B C D
7	A B C D
8	A B C D

PART 2: Write your answers clearly IN CAPITAL LETTERS. Write one letter in each box.

9	
10	
11	
12	
13	
14	
15	
16	

PART 3: Write your answers clearly IN CAPITAL LETTERS. Write one letter in each box.

17	
18	
19	
20	
21	
22	
23	
24	

PART 4: Write only the missing words IN CAPITAL LETTERS.

25	
26	
27	
28	
29	
30	

PART 5: Mark ONE letter for each question.

31	A B C D
32	A B C D
33	A B C D

34	A B C D
35	A B C D
36	A B C D

PART 6: Mark ONE letter for each question.

37	A	B	C	D	E	F	G
38	A	B	C	D	E	F	G
39	A	B	C	D	E	F	G

40	A	B	C	D	E	F	G
41	A	B	C	D	E	F	G
42	A	B	C	D	E	F	G

PART 7: Mark ONE letter for each question.

43	A	B	C	D
44	A	B	C	D
45	A	B	C	D
46	A	B	C	D
47	A	B	C	D

48	A	B	C	D
49	A	B	C	D
50	A	B	C	D
51	A	B	C	D
52	A	B	C	D

LISTENING

PART 1: Mark ONE letter for each question.

1	A	B	C
2	A	B	C
3	A	B	C
4	A	B	C

5	A	B	C
6	A	B	C
7	A	B	C
8	A	B	C

PART 2: Write your answers clearly IN CAPITAL LETTERS. Write one letter in each box.

9														
10														
11														
12														
13														
14														
15														
16														
17														
18														

PART 3: Mark ONE letter for each question.

19	A	B	C	D	E	F	G	H
20	A	B	C	D	E	F	G	H
21	A	B	C	D	E	F	G	H
22	A	B	C	D	E	F	G	H
23	A	B	C	D	E	F	G	H

PART 4: Mark ONE letter for each question.

24	A	B	C
25	A	B	C
26	A	B	C
27	A	B	C

28	A	B	C
29	A	B	C
30	A	B	C

Assessing the Writing paper

Students' answers are assessed using a mark scheme which was developed with close reference to the Common European Framework of Reference for Languages (CEFR). Marks are awarded from 0 to 5 on each of the following four scales:

Content focuses on how well the candidate has fulfilled the task, in other words if they have done what they were asked to do.

Communicative achievement focuses on how appropriate the writing is for the task and whether the candidate has used the appropriate register.

Organization focuses on the way the candidate puts together the piece of writing, in other words if it is logical and ordered.

Language focuses on vocabulary and grammar. This includes the range of language as well as how accurate it is.

Tasks on the *Cambridge English: First* Writing paper are assessed using the following scale, based on B2 of the CEFR:

B2	Content	Communicative Achievement	Organization	Language
5	All content is relevant to the task. Target reader is fully informed.	Uses the conventions of the communicative task effectively to hold the target reader's attention and communicate straightforward and complex ideas, as appropriate.	Text is well-organized and coherent, using a variety of cohesive devices and organizational patterns to generally good effect.	Uses a range of vocabulary, including less common lexis, appropriately. Uses a range of simple and complex grammatical forms with control and flexibility. Occasional errors may be present but do not impede communication.
4	*Performance shares features of Bands 3 and 5.*			
3	Minor irrelevances and/or omissions may be present. Target reader is on the whole informed.	Uses the conventions of the communicative task to hold the target reader's attention and communicate straightforward ideas.	Text is generally well-organized and coherent, using a variety of linking words and cohesive devices.	Uses a range of everyday vocabulary appropriately, with occasional inappropriate use of less common lexis. Uses a range of simple and some complex grammatical forms with a good degree of control. Errors do not impede communication.
2	*Performance shares features of Bands 1 and 3.*			
1	Irrelevances and misinterpretation of task may be present. Target reader is minimally informed.	Uses the conventions of the communicative task in generally appropriate ways to communicate straightforward ideas.	Text is connected and coherent, using basic linking words and a limited number of cohesive devices.	Uses everyday vocabulary generally appropriately, while occasionally overusing certain lexis. Uses simple grammatical forms with a good degree of control. While errors are noticeable, meaning can still be determined.
0	Content is totally irrelevant. Target reader is not informed.	*Performance below Band 1*		

Assessing the Speaking paper

Assessment is based on performance in the whole test, and is not related to performance in particular parts of the test. Students are assessed on their own performance, and not in relation to each other.

Marks are awarded by the assessor, who does not take part in the test, according to four analytical criteria:

- *Grammar and Vocabulary*
- *Pronunciation*
- *Discourse Management*
- *Interactive Communication*

The interlocutor, who conducts the test, gives a mark for *Global Achievement*.

B2	Grammar and vocabulary	Discourse management	Pronunciation	Interactive communication
5	Shows a good degree of control of a range of simple and some complex grammatical forms. Uses a range of appropriate vocabulary to give and exchange views on a wide range of familiar topics.	Produces extended stretches of language with very little hesitation. Contributions are relevant and there is a clear organization of ideas. Uses a range of cohesive devices and discourse markers.	Is intelligible. Intonation is appropriate. Sentence and word stress is accurately placed. Individual sounds are articulated clearly.	Initiates and responds appropriately, linking contributions to those of other speakers. Maintains and develops the interaction and negotiates towards an outcome.
4	*Performance shares features of Bands 3 and 5.*			
3	Shows a good degree of control of simple grammatical forms, and attempts some complex grammatical forms. Uses a range of appropriate vocabulary to give and exchange views on a range of familiar topics.	Produces extended stretches of language despite some hesitation. Contributions are relevant and there is very little repetition. Uses a range of cohesive devices.	Is intelligible. Intonation is generally appropriate. Sentence and word stress is generally accurately placed. Individual sounds are generally articulated clearly.	Initiates and responds appropriately. Maintains and develops the interaction and negotiates towards an outcome with very little support.
2	*Performance shares features of Bands 1 and 3.*			
1	Shows a good degree of control of simple and grammatical forms. Uses a range of appropriate vocabulary when talking about everyday situations.	Produces responses which are extended beyond short phrases, despite hesitation. Contributions are mostly relevant, despite some repetition. Uses basic cohesive devices.	Is mostly intelligible, and has some control of phonological features at both utterance and word levels.	Initiates and responds appropriately. Keeps the interaction going with very little prompting and support.
0	*Performance below Band 1.*			

B2	Global Achievement
5	Handles communication on a range of familiar topics, with very little hesitation. Uses accurate and appropriate linguistic resources to express ideas and produce extended discourse that is generally coherent.
4	*Performance shares features of Bands 3 and 5.*
3	Handles communication on familiar topics, despite some hesitation. Organizes extended discourse but occasionally produces utterances that lack coherence, and some inaccuracies and inappropriate usage occur.
2	*Performance shares features of Bands 1 and 3.*
1	Handles communication in everyday situations, despite hesitation. Constructs longer utterances but is not able to use complex language except in well-rehearsed utterances.
0	*Performance below Band 1.*

QUESTION 4

Mark scheme

Content

The review should describe the programme briefly and explain what the writer dislikes about it.

Communicative achievement

The review can be informal or neutral. The notice indicates that the review should contain a totally personal reaction to a programme and that it might be amusing. The reader should have a clear idea of what the programme is like and why the writer dislikes it so much.

Organization

The review may be divided into paragraphs, beginning with a description of the programme itself and then giving the writer's opinions of it. It may have a title (probably the name of the programme). Linking words and phrases should be used appropriately, particularly to link the writer's opinions with the reasons for them.

Language

The review should include appropriate structures for giving opinions and for expressing dislike. It should also include appropriate vocabulary for describing TV programmes (e.g. the people in them, what happens in them, etc.).

Model answer

INSIDE THE HOUSE

In my opinion this programme is the worst thing on TV at the moment and I simply cannot understand why anyone would want to watch it. In the programme, a group of young people who have never met each other before are sent to live in a big house in the middle of the countryside. The programme shows you how they get on with each other.

The main problem with this programme is that all the people in it are awful. They are all obviously desperate to be famous by appearing on TV but they are not interesting people at all. They talk about themselves all the time but they have very annoying personalities and their opinions are stupid. They are completely selfish and although they seem to think people watching them will find them fascinating, in fact I'm sure everyone at home is saying how terrible they are.

Another thing that makes the programme so annoying is that the people argue with each other all the time. It makes me just want to tell them all to shut up!

Listening

PART 1

1	B	5	A
2	A	6	C
3	C	7	A
4	A	8	C

PART 2

9	social	14	ten/10 minutes
10	width	15	long; heavy
11	handler	16	lie down
12	pick up	17	attitude
13	nine/9	18	their ears

PART 3

19	A	22	D
20	G	23	E
21	H		

PART 4

24	B	28	A
25	A	29	C
26	B	30	A
27	C		

Each correct answer receives 1 mark.

Speaking

Teachers should use their own judgement to award marks based on the assessment criteria on page 95.

TEST 2

Reading and Use of English

PART 1

1	B	4	B	7	B
2	D	5	A	8	A
3	B	6	B		

PART 2

9	back/backward(s)	13	for
10	As/When	14	and
11	so	15	most
12	together	16	why

PART 3

17	stressful	21	memorable
18	solution	22	helpful
19	accompanies	23	insights
20	personal	24	truly

PART 4

25 **instead** of][buying her a
26 is being][**run** by
27 does it][**take** (you) to
28 were][no tickets **left OR** weren't][any tickets **left**
29 there is][a **sudden**
30 has never been][**happier** than

PART 5

31 C   34 B
32 C   35 D
33 A   36 B

PART 6

37 E   40 A
38 C   41 D
39 G   42 F

PART 7

43 C   47 B   51 B
44 B   48 C   52 C
45 D   49 C
46 A   50 D

Parts **1–3** = 1 mark for each correct answer
Part **4** = up to 2 marks for each correct answer
Parts **5–6** = 2 marks for each correct answer
Part **7** = 1 mark for each correct answer

Writing

For assessment information see page 94.

QUESTION 1

Mark scheme

Content

The essay should fully address the question, discussing different news topics and comparing how important these are to people in general.

Communicative achievement

The essay should be fairly formal or neutral. The reader should understand fully the points the writer makes and the reasons given to support those points.

Organization

The essay should be appropriately divided into paragraphs, perhaps with a different paragraph for each of the three areas in the notes. A short introductory paragraph may be included but is not compulsory. Appropriate linking between different points should be used (e.g. *whereas*).

Language

It is likely that modal verbs such as *can*, *might*, *may*, etc. are required to talk about possible situations and the results of them. The present simple tense is likely

to be required to talk about habits and general facts. Vocabulary connected with the media, different kinds of news and people's feelings is required.

Model answer

Some people are very interested in the news and keep up to date with it all the time, whereas other people pay little attention to it.

A lot of things in the news are about politics. People who are interested in politics can be influenced by what they read or see in the news but usually the news does not change their opinions. They have certain beliefs anyway and these beliefs affect how they respond to political news – they are pleased or angry, depending on what the politicians are doing.

News of crime may have a big influence on people who read about it in the news. This is because it can increase their fear of crime and make them think that they could be a victim of it. Particularly, stories about local crime can affect people a lot.

These days, the kind of news that has the most influence on people seems to be news about famous people. The media are full of news about celebrities and this seems to be much more important to a lot of people than news about politics, crime, economics, wars or any other serious subject.

QUESTION 2

Mark scheme

Content

The report should describe events and changes in the place. It may refer to people in general or to specific people. It should include facts and it may also include comments on the events.

Communicative achievement

The report should be fairly formal or neutral, because it deals mostly with facts and because the topic is a fairly serious one. The reader should understand what kind of place is being described and what some of the most important events and changes were in that place in the last year. The reader may also understand the writer's opinions of these events.

Organization

The report may be divided into appropriate sections, each dealing with a different aspect. To make the report absolutely clear at a glance, these sections may be given titles, and the whole report may be given a title. Appropriate and varied use of linking words and phrases may be required (e.g. *This ...* , *However*, etc.)

Language

The appropriate verb tenses should be used for describing past events and perhaps present situations resulting from them. Passive verb forms are likely to be required, because what happened may be more important than who did it. Comparative structures may be required. Appropriate vocabulary associated with the type of event described is required.

Model answer

A YEAR IN THE LIFE OF PARKSIDE

Shopping

The most important event in the last year was probably the opening of the new shopping centre. It took some years for it to be built, but it finally opened in July. Most local people are very happy with it because we now have bigger shops than we used to have. However, other people say that it is not a good thing because some of the smaller shops in the town will have to close because of the new shopping centre.

Sport

Our football team did very well last season and got to the final of the National Cup competition. Thousands of us travelled to the National Stadium for the match and it was a fantastic day for the town. The team lost, but getting to the final for the first time was a great achievement for them.

Traffic

A new traffic system was introduced last year because the number of cars in the town centre had become too great and there was a lot of congestion. This has worked well and there are now fewer traffic jams in the centre.

QUESTION 3

Mark scheme

Content

The article should describe the club, saying what the writer does as a member of it and explain why the writer likes being a member of the club.

Communicative achievement

The article can be fairly informal or neutral. The reader should be clear about the club and its activities and also understand clearly why the writer enjoys being a member.

Organization

The article should be organized into clear paragraphs dealing separately with what the club is and does, and why the writer likes being a member. It could also have an introductory paragraph explain why the writer joined the club, as well as a suitable title. Appropriate linking words and phrases for connecting pieces of information and points should be used.

Language

The article should use a range of appropriate verb tenses and a range of suitable grammatical structures, with sentences that are not all very short and simple. Vocabulary connected with the topic area of the club chosen must be used appropriately.

Model answer

MY BOOK CLUB

I belong to a book club that meets once a month at the home of the person who founded it about a year ago. I heard about it from a friend of mine who is also a member. She told me that I would really enjoy being in the club and she was right.

At each meeting, we discuss a book that we have all read during the month before the meeting. We talk about what we liked or disliked about it, we analyse the plot and the characters and we discuss the writer's style. The meetings are always really interesting for me.

There are two main reasons why joining the book club has been good for me. Firstly, it has taught me a lot, because I have read books that I would not have read if I wasn't a member. This means I have widened my knowledge of literature and discovered new authors I had not known about before. Secondly, the social aspect is a great advantage and I have made some fantastic new friends.

If you like reading, join a book club – you'll be very pleased that you did.

QUESTION 4

Mark scheme

Content

The letter must name the person the writer would like to interview, say why the writer wants to interview that person and give examples of questions the writer would ask that person.

Communicative achievement

The register may be neutral or fairly informal. The letter is to a magazine, not to an individual that the writer knows, and therefore it should not be too informal. However, the subject matter and situation mean that it should not be too formal. The reader would understand clearly why the writer has chosen the person and what the writer would ask the person in an interview.

Organization

The letter may be divided into paragraphs dealing separately with the person chosen and the reason for that choice, and the questions to ask that person. Appropriate linking words and phrases should be used to link the writer's choices of person and questions with the reasons for those choices. The questions may be presented as a list, linked with words such as *also* and *Finally*.

Language

The letter should use appropriate past and present tenses to talk about the person the writer would like to interview. Conditional structures are also likely to be required, and the modal *would* is likely to be required to talk about the hypothetical situation of interviewing the person.

Vocabulary appropriate to the kind of person chosen (e.g. their work) is required and vocabulary connected with describing someone's personality may be required.

Model answer

To the Editor,

The person I would really like to interview is the actress Gloria Johnson.

I would really like to interview her because I think she is the greatest actress in films today. I have seen all the films that she has starred in and I think that she is better than anyone else. Also, she has played a wide variety of roles in her films, and she has shown that she is a great actress in all of them. You believe that she really is that person in all her films.

If I could interview her, I would ask her about how she chooses which films she is going to appear in and how she prepares for each role. I would ask her what her favourite role has been. I would also like to know which actors she has enjoyed acting with and which ones she has not enjoyed acting with. Finally, I would ask her a few questions about her private life. She never talks about that in the interviews I've read but I hope that she would talk to me about it!

Yours sincerely,

Listening

PART 1

1 B	4 A	7 C
2 A	5 A	8 B
3 B	6 B	

PART 2

9 underground systems	14 ear plugs
10 hairdryer	15 two-minute/2-minute
11 glass	16 ball of air
12 elbows; knees	17 smile machine
13 over/more than four/4	18 body flying

PART 3

19 E	21 A	23 F
20 H	22 D	

PART 4

24 C	28 A
25 A	29 B
26 B	30 C
27 B	

Each correct answer receives 1 mark.

Speaking

Teachers should use their own judgement to award marks based on the assessment information on page 95.

TEST 3

Reading and Use of English

PART 1

1 B	5 B
2 A	6 C
3 D	7 A
4 A	8 B

PART 2

9 which/that	12 too	15 those
10 as	13 enough	16 well
11 having	14 if/should	

PART 3

17 coincidence	21 birth
18 conversation	22 exactly
19 discoveries	23 engagement
20 wedding(s)	24 unbelievable

PART 4

25 has a **tendency**][to behave
26 **twice** as][much (money) as
27 **made** me][lose my
28 so **much**][skill
29 as a **result**][of getting
30 **ran** into][a friend of

PART 5

31 B	34 D
32 D	35 A
33 A	36 C

PART 6

37 F	40 G
38 C	41 D
39 A	42 E

PART 7

43 B	47 C	51 B
44 D	48 D	52 C
45 A	49 B	
46 A	50 A	

Parts 1–3 = 1 mark for each correct answer
Part 4 = up to 2 marks for each correct answer
Parts 5–6 = 2 marks for each correct answer
Part 7 = 1 mark for each correct answer

Writing

For assessment information see page 94.

QUESTION 1

Mark scheme

Content

The essay should fully address the question, discussing why sport plays such an important role in a great many people's lives. Aspects of sport that are not relevant to the question should not be included.

Communicative achievement

The essay should be fairly formal or neutral. The reader should understand fully the points the writer makes and the reasons given to support those points.

Organization

The essay should be appropriately divided into paragraphs, perhaps with a different paragraph for each of the three areas in the notes. Appropriate linking words and phrases should be used for linking views with reasons that support those views (e.g. *Firstly, Secondly,* etc.).

Language

The present simple tense is likely to be required to talk about regular activities and general facts, and conditional structures may be required to talk about possibilities and the results of them. Vocabulary connected with both playing and watching sports, and feelings, is required.

Model answer

For some people, sport is a very important thing in life. If they play a sport, it is good for them in different ways. Firstly, it has big health benefits, since people who regularly do sports tend to be fitter and healthier than people who don't. Secondly, sport is good for social reasons. If you are a member of a club, you can make new friends and if you play a team sport, you can also enjoy doing something that involves getting on well with others and working together in order to win.

A lot of people who don't play sports get a lot of pleasure from watching them on television and going to games. Some football supporters, for example, have a great passion for the team they support and this can affect their lives a lot – they get very happy if the team wins and very depressed if the team loses.

One reason why sport is important to such a lot of people is that it takes their minds away from everyday life, from work and any problems they may have in their lives. Sport gives them relaxation and joy.

QUESTION 2

Mark scheme

Content

The review should describe what the show consisted of and contain the writer's opinions and reactions to the performance(s).

Communicative achievement

The review can be informal or neutral. The reader should have a clear idea of what the show was like and what the writer thought of it.

Organization

The review may be divided into paragraphs, beginning with a description of the whole show and then giving the writer's opinions of it, or each paragraph could deal with parts of the show and the writer's comments on them. Linking words and phrases should be used appropriately to link both factual descriptions and opinions.

Language

The review should include appropriate structures for describing a programme of events and performances in it and for describing reactions and giving opinions. A range of appropriate past verb tenses, probably including the passive, should be used accurately. The review should also include appropriate vocabulary for the kind(s) of performance described and for commenting on a show.

Model answer

THE ANNUAL SHOW

Every year, the college's annual show enables people to see how much talent there is at the college. This year's show was another excellent one, and it included music, comedy and poetry.

For me, the musical highlight was the performance of Camille Clarke, whose folk songs greatly impressed everyone who was there. The audience listened in complete silence to her wonderful voice and applauded wildly at the end. There were other fantastic musical performances too, including those by the rock band The Magic and the classical piano of Tom Croft.

Comedy was supplied by Michelle Dyer and George Little, who had very different styles, Michelle focusing on the small things in everyday life and George commenting on the things that happen at the college. Both of them were very funny and made the audience laugh a lot.

Helen Dodd's poetry was also very well received, grabbing the audience's attention because of how well it was written and spoken.

The standard of all the performances was extremely high and the whole evening was very enjoyable from start to finish. Well done, everyone!

QUESTION 3

Mark scheme

Content

The article must include all the aspects listed – what the hobby involves, why the writer likes it, why the writer started it, and how long the writer spends doing it.

Communicative achievement

The article can be fairly informal or neutral – the announcement indicates this. It is for other people's entertainment. The reader should understand exactly what the hobby involves and why the writer enjoys it.

Organization

The article should be organized so that each of the aspects listed is dealt with in a logical order – this does not have to be the same order as in the question. Different aspects may be separated into different paragraphs. Appropriate linking words and phrases should be used to connect different aspects, to describe sequences of events and to give reasons.

Language

The article must use appropriate verb tenses – probably the present simple for what the hobby involves and perhaps the present perfect for the situation until now, as well as the past simple for the history of the hobby. Vocabulary connected with the hobby must be used accurately.

Model answer

My favourite hobby is collecting the autographs of famous people. I've got over 200 autographs at the moment, and I've collected the signatures of all sorts of famous people – sports people, actors, musicians and TV stars. I go to lots of events that famous people are attending and I wait in the best place, for example the entrance to a building – and I ask the person to sign their name in my book when they are going in or out. I love it because I can speak to famous people and then I can look at my collection and show it to other people.

I started the hobby when I was walking past a hotel in the city centre one day and a very famous pop star suddenly came out. I asked her for her autograph. She signed her name on a piece of paper and that was my first autograph. After that, I wanted to collect more autographs and it became my main hobby. Now I spend most weekends trying to get more autographs.

QUESTION 4

Mark scheme

Content

The report should describe one or more fashions among young people in the place where the writer lives. It does not have to describe any of the fashions listed in the question because candidates are told they can describe any fashion they choose. The report must also contain the writer's opinion(s).

Communicative achievement

The report may be fairly formal or neutral if the candidate is talking about something they regard as fairly serious. On the other hand, the report may be quite informal, to entertain or amuse the reader. The reader should understand exactly what the fashion or fashions involve (and the reader may know nothing about the fashion(s) before reading the report). The reader should also understand what the writer thinks of the fashion(s).

Organization

If more than one fashion is described, the report should be divided into appropriate sections, probably with a title for each section. If a single fashion is described, the report may be in the form of a single paragraph. The whole report may be given a title. Appropriate linking words and phrases should be used (e.g. *For example* to introduce an example of young people following a particular fashion).

Language

The fashion must be described using the appropriate present tense(s). Appropriate vocabulary connected with the chosen fashion(s) is required, as well as appropriate structures and vocabulary for giving opinions.

Model answer

FASHIONABLE PHRASES

The latest fashion among young people in the place where I live is connected with a TV programme that's very popular at the moment. The programme is called 'Bleep' and it's a drama series about the lives of various teenagers. It's supposed to be funny and the characters in it all use certain phrases all the time. People copy the phrases these characters use and they say them all the time. If you don't watch the programme, you don't know what people are talking about now. People whisper these phrases in class and then everyone laughs, or they say them to each other in the street and then they all start laughing. It's like some kind of special language that they all use now. For example, one character in the programme is always saying 'You must be mad'. People say that all the time now, even when it doesn't make sense. Personally, I think this is a pretty silly fashion. I like the programme, but I don't understand why everyone keeps saying these things and then laughing. They must be mad!

Listening

PART 1

1	C	4	A	7	A
2	B	5	C	8	A
3	B	6	A		

PART 2

9 landowners
10 contract
11 facilities
12 (the) weather
13 agents
14 voting
15 volunteers
16 security
17 promoting
18 advance tickets

PART 3

19	H	22	C
20	B	23	A
21	F		

PART 4

24	C	27	A	29	A
25	C	28	B	30	C
26	B				

Each correct answer receives 1 mark.

Speaking

Teachers should use their own judgement to award marks based on the assessment criteria on page 95.

TEST 4

Reading and Use of English

PART 1

1	A	4	A	7	B
2	C	5	C	8	C
3	D	6	B		

PART 2

9	which	13	than
10	for	14	being
11	a	15	as
12	is	16	so

PART 3

17	invitations/invites	21	attention
18	dislike	22	techniques
19	advice	23	ensures
20	listeners	24	legendary

PART 4

25 we're/we are **supposed**][to reply
26 must have][**left** it
27 to **catch**][on
28 of][at **least**
29 doesn't/does not **know**][how to
30 made][a **note** of

PART 5

31	A	34	B
32	C	35	C
33	D	36	D

PART 6

37	E	40	D
38	G	41	B
39	A	42	F

PART 7

43	E	47	F	51	B
44	D	48	C	52	E
45	C	49	D		
46	A	50	D		

Parts 1–3 = 1 mark for each correct answer
Part 4 = up to 2 marks for each correct answer
Parts 5–6 = 2 marks for each correct answer
Part 7 = 1 mark for each correct answer

Writing

For assessment information see page 94.

QUESTION 1

Mark scheme

Content

The essay should fully address the point made in the statement, and not include points that are not directly relevant to that. The writer may agree or disagree, or both agree and disagree.

Communicative achievement

The essay should be fairly formal or neutral. The reader must fully understand the writer's opinions on the topic and the reasons why the writer has those opinions.

Organization

The essay may be divided into appropriate paragraphs, each one making separate general points, or it may also be organized into one paragraph of agreement with the statement and one of disagreement. Appropriate linking words and phrases should be used for linking points made and opinions expressed.

Language

It is likely that modal verbs (e.g. *should*, *can*, *might*, etc.) will be required to give views on what people are and are not able to do, and what is good for people. The present simple verb tense is required to talk about general situations. Conditional structures may be required to talk about possible situations and the results of them. Vocabulary connected with work and making decisions should be used accurately.

Model answer

In many countries in modern times it is not necessary to decide what kind of career you are going to have until you are older. These days lots of people change their careers many times through their lives. In the past, most people had to choose a career when they were young and then stay in that career for all of their working lives. Nowadays, it's possible to try different careers before you decide on the one you want to concentrate on. This is a good thing, because it gives people more freedom. They can decide on their career when they are older and have more experience of life. This means that they are more likely to choose a career they enjoy.

On the other hand, it is important to decide on some careers when you are still quite young, because it is harder to start those careers when you are older. If you want to be a doctor, or an architect, or have any career that requires many years of training, you need to make your decision when you are still quite young.

QUESTION 2

Mark scheme

Content

The review should give a brief summary of the game and the writer's opinions of it, with reasons.

Communicative achievement

The review should be neutral or informal – the factual description may be neutral and the opinions informal. The reader should get a clear general idea of what the game involves and should understand what the writer thinks of the game.

Organization

The review should be organized appropriately into paragraphs providing factual information on the game and opinions of it.

Language

The review should use appropriate structures for describing a game, including the appropriate present tense(s) for describing what you do and appropriate modal verbs (*must, have to, can't*, etc.) for describing the rules. Appropriate structures for giving opinions should also be used. Vocabulary appropriate for the game chosen should be used accurately.

Model answer

MONOPOLY

I recently played a game of Monopoly, which is one of the oldest board games in the world. You can buy different versions of it in different countries.

Basically, the game is about buying different properties that are on the board. You throw dice and move around the board and you can choose to buy properties that you land on. If you land on a property that belongs to another player, you have to pay them. Everyone gets a certain amount of money at the start, and if you have no money left, you're out of the game.

The game is quite good fun, and to be good at it you have to think about what the best strategy is. You have to think like a business person. I think it's been popular for so long because it's easy to play but also quite interesting because it's not too simple.

The only problem with Monopoly is that it can take a very long time to play the game, and so it can become quite boring.

QUESTION 3

Mark scheme

Content

The letter should explain what the competition or tournament was, describe the writer's experience when he/she entered it, and describe the writer's feelings about the experience.

Communicative achievement

The letter may be neutral or fairly informal. It is for a magazine, not an individual that the writer knows, but the announcement is asking for personal experiences and so the letter should not be too formal. The reader should understand clearly what the writer entered, what happened and how the writer felt about it or feels about it now.

Organization

The letter may be divided into paragraphs, dealing with the general background, the actual experience and the writer's feelings. It should clearly describe the sequence of events. Appropriate linking should be used for each part of the sequence of events and for linking the events with the writer's feelings about them.

Language

The letter should use appropriate past tenses for describing the experience (the past simple and perhaps past continuous and past perfect tenses). Vocabulary appropriate to the sport or type of competition should be used accurately, as well as vocabulary for describing feelings.

Model answer

To the Editor,

Last year I entered a regional tennis tournament. I was in the under-17 age group and the tournament took place at the biggest tennis club in the area. I didn't expect to do very well in the tournament but I decided to enter and see what happened.

When I got to the club, I was quite nervous because I had never played at such a big club. When I was getting changed before my first game, all the other players seemed much more confident than me.

I won my first game and I was really pleased about that. It made me much more confident and then I won my next game too. Eventually I reached the semi-final, but I lost that game. The other player was much better than me. She won the tournament and people say she's one of the best players in the country in that age group.

After the tournament I was very proud of what I had achieved and I realized that I am a good player. I'm planning to enter more tournaments now.

Yours sincerely,

QUESTION 4

Mark scheme

Content

The report should describe the situation regarding tourism in the place where the writer lives, including details of tourist attractions.

Communicative achievement

The report should be fairly formal or neutral. The reader should be clear about what attracts tourists/why tourists do not visit the place, and what is available for tourists.

Organization

The report should be divided into logical and clear paragraphs, each dealing with a different aspect of tourism in the place (e.g. tourist numbers, tourist attractions, facilities for tourists, etc.). The report may have a suitable title and each section may also have a title but this is not essential. Appropriate linking words and phrases should be used, e.g. to give examples and to connect related points and pieces of information.

Language

Appropriate verb tenses should be used for describing the situation, and a range of suitable grammatical structures should be used, e.g. relative clauses for giving information about places and aspects of tourism. Appropriate vocabulary connected with the topic of tourism is required.

Model answer

TOURISM IN THE CITY

Tourist numbers & publicity

This city is not a particularly popular place in the country for tourists to visit. However, some tourists do come here and the number has been increasing. The city authorities have been trying to attract more visitors and they are having success in doing this, with publicity that focuses on how inexpensive it is to stay in hotels here.

Main tourist attractions

The main attraction of the city is its old buildings, particularly the cathedral, which every visitor goes to. Guided tours of the building are very popular and there are often queues for these. The Grey House is also popular with tourists – this is an old house that has been turned into a museum which shows how people in the city lived over two hundred years ago. In the area which is the old city centre, there are also other interesting old buildings which tourists like to photograph.

Other attractions

Apart from the history of the city, another feature which attracts some tourists is the market, which is mentioned in all the guidebooks because it has a reputation for both high-quality goods and bargains.

Listening

PART 1

1	C	4	B	7	B
2	B	5	B	8	A
3	C	6	A		

PART 2

9	loan	14	socially responsible
10	an engineer	15	multiple entries
11	poorest people	16	script
12	one/1 minute	17	passion
13	product; service	18	ten/10

PART 3

19	F	22	B
20	C	23	D
21	A		

PART 4

24	A	28	B
25	C	29	B
26	A	30	C
27	A		

Each correct answer receives 1 mark.

Speaking

Teachers should use their own judgement to award marks based on the assessment criteria on page 95.

TEST 1

Part One.
You will hear people talking in eight different situations. For questions 1–8, choose the best answer, A, B or C.

ONE.
You hear someone talking about football referees.

Man: You have to feel sorry for referees. I mean, they're under terrible pressure throughout the game, with players shouting at them, and cheating and all that. And of course, the fans of both sides give them a hard time – they just can't win. Sure, they make mistakes, plenty of them, but they're only human. They don't go out there thinking, 'I'm going to do really badly today,' they're doing their best. Some people think that there are referees who just want to draw attention to themselves, who think they're as important as the players, but that's not my view. I mean, who'd want their job, with all that criticism all the time? *repeat extract 1*

TWO.
You hear a famous chef talking about his week.

Chef: I had a bit of an odd week. I went to Birmingham to do a TV cookery show. I had to make my special recipe pancakes, but the pan they gave me in the studio wasn't nearly big enough, so it made things all a bit difficult. But it turned out all right in the end, they were just a bit smaller than usual! Later in the week I was on a radio show answering listeners' questions about cooking, and then I did a few interviews about my new book. *repeat extract 2*

THREE.
You hear someone talking about her career in dancing.

Woman: I just had to dance. When I was a girl, I was always putting on dancing shows for my parents. By the time I was seven I knew what I wanted to be, and that feeling never went away. I told my parents I wanted to do proper ballet. So I went to a ballet school and I've been dancing ever since. I used to have classes after school and on Saturdays. And, when I finished school, I went to a full-time dance academy for four years. Now I'm teaching dance, and I've never been happier. *repeat extract 3*

FOUR.
You hear someone talking on the phone at work.

Woman: So what time are you going to make it? You know it's a very important meeting and we can't really discuss the issue properly without you. Yes, I'll tell her you'll get here as soon as you can, but I know she isn't going to be very pleased. OK, I'll delay things as long as I can – I'll say you've got problems at home or something. No, I won't say you've overslept, I don't want to get you in trouble. *repeat extract 4*

FIVE.
You hear a radio presenter talking about a book.

Presenter: Have you ever wondered how many tons of food you eat in a lifetime, or how many miles of blood vessels there are in your body? No? Oh well, there are plenty more intriguing entries in this huge book of facts. It claims to have the most accurate and up-to-date information about every subject on Earth. I'm not sure it covers absolutely everything, but it certainly has lots of fascinating facts on pretty much any topic you can think of – you won't be able to put it down! *repeat extract 5*

SIX.
You hear part of an interview with a famous comedian.

Interviewer: What was your favourite subject at school?

Man: Maths, by far. I loved it, so I was good at it. I couldn't get enthusiastic about other subjects, but with maths I wanted to show off. I liked the logic of it.

Interviewer: Were you a good student?

Man: Yes, pretty much. I didn't cause a lot of trouble or anything like that. I was cheeky and I liked having a laugh with my friends, but I always managed to make the teachers laugh before they told me off. All in all, I had a great time at school. *repeat extract 6*

SEVEN.
You hear someone talking about a person he knows.

Man: I really don't see why I have to keep doing him favours. He never does any for me. I guess you were right about him all along – you always said he took advantage of other people. I didn't believe you then but now I can see what you mean. I can see now that I was totally wrong about him. It's a real shame, because I thought we were great friends for a while. But I'm just not going to put up with him any longer. I mean, he surely can't expect to behave like that and get away with it. *repeat extract 7*

EIGHT.
You hear a tour guide talking to a group of visitors at a museum.

Guide: OK, that's the end of my introductory talk and now you can wander around on your own for a couple of hours. We'll meet back here at 12.30. Before you go, a bit of advice. This is an enormous museum, packed full of fascinating things, and you can't expect to see it all in one go. So, if I were you I'd concentrate on one or two sections and look at them in detail. Have a look at the map – you've all got one and it's very simple and clear – and decide where you want to go. And split up into couples or small groups – it gets pretty crowded here and you won't have much fun if a lot of you try to stick together. *repeat extract 8*

That is the end of Part One. Now turn to Part Two.

You will hear someone talking about the sport of elephant polo. For questions 9–18, complete the sentences with a word or short phrase. You now have 45 seconds to look at Part 2.

Elephant polo player: Of course, polo is normally played on horses, and it's a very fast game. Well, we don't claim that elephant polo is the fastest game in the world, but we always maintain it's the biggest. The elephants do actually enjoy polo. Definitely. It's a lot of fun for them because they're social animals, and a polo tournament is a week when dozens of elephants meet up, many from the same family, like a reunion. And of course they get fed extremely well – better than in their normal life. They use up a lot of energy and get through masses of sugar cane, especially at half-time.

The players sit on elephants and hit a white wooden ball, using a long bamboo stick that has a polo mallet head on the end of it. The pitch is about three-quarters the length of a football pitch, and the goals are the same width as football goals. There's a basic saddle and the players are strapped onto the elephants. We've never had a serious accident. A mahout – an elephant handler – sits behind each player and guides the elephant. Sometimes the mahouts have their own games, guiding the elephant and hitting the ball as well. That takes incredible skill.

During a game, if the ball hits an elephant, that's fine. Their legs are quite thick and they do get in the way. Quite often they will kick the ball so that they can run after it. They're not allowed to pick up the ball with their trunks, though they sometimes try. That would be a free hit to the other side.

There are four elephants per team in a tournament, plus the referee's elephant – that's nine on the pitch at any one time. We usually have sixteen animals available on any given day, in four teams. There are two halves, called chukkas, in a game of elephant polo, the same as in normal polo. We play ten minutes of actual play. Whenever the whistle blows, the clock stops. A novice team might score one or two goals, if they're lucky, while an advanced team might score about ten.

The polo rules are that a man can only hold the stick with his right arm, even if he is left-handed. Women can use both hands. Using the stick is hard work, because it's long and the head is heavy. By the end of the game, your arm will be aching. But it's an easy game to pick up with a little practice.

During the game, you chase after the ball on your elephant, going quite quickly, and you can easily miss it, though the elephant will often help you out with his foot. The elephants usually supply the entertainment. They might decide to lie down across the goal for fun but that's an absolute no-no.

Ultimately it's about elephants charging up and down the pitch, scoring great goals themselves and having a lot of fun. If the elephants didn't enjoy it, or if there was any form of misbehaving, they would be removed from the game – sent off, if you like. It's not worth risking an elephant with an attitude problem.

You get all sorts. You get big elephants that are a bit older and wiser, and we use a lot of small ones that can be exceptionally quick. We try to remove what you might call the elephant factor by swapping elephants and mahouts with the other team at half-time. If you've got elephants that don't normally live together, there can be some tension. The sport always uses Indian elephants. The problem with African ones is that their ears get in the way. And they're much taller.

In the exam you will hear the recording twice. To listen again now, go to the beginning of the track.

That is the end of Part Two. Now turn to Part Three.

You will hear five different people talking about cities they have visited. For questions 19–23, choose from the list A–H the opinion each person gives about the city. Use the letters only once. There are three extra letters which you do not need to use. You now have 30 seconds to look at Part Three.

Speaker 1: The place is always on TV and in films and in magazines, and so you get a mental picture of what it's like even if you haven't been there. You have this image of skyscrapers everywhere, streets full of traffic and people, everyone rushing around, talking fast and leading busy lives. You think of it as having a real buzz. And guess what? It was just like that. Everything I'd expected to find was there. In fact, it all seemed so familiar that it was as if I'd actually been there before.

Speaker 2: I discovered after I'd been there that you need to be really careful about when you choose to visit the place. There are very busy times and quieter times. Without realizing it, I chose one of the busy times, and wow, was it busy! The place was packed, and of course with the narrow streets it is famed for, that makes movement difficult. I just shuffled along with everyone else, going at their pace, so I didn't manage to see much. There's a great atmosphere there, and of course it looks wonderful, but I could have done with a bit more room to move. So I guess I didn't see it at its best.

Speaker 3: Everyone I've met who's been there says what a fantastic place it is, and I was expecting something really special. And I wasn't disappointed, though I must say the picture I'd had of it in my mind didn't turn out to be totally accurate. In fact, it not only lived up to my expectations, it exceeded them. People always associate it with its famous buildings, but it was the less well-known places that struck me. In every little street, especially away from the tourist areas, there was something fascinating to see. It's those little streets that were really memorable for me.

Speaker 4: I'd been looking forward to going there for a long time and I finally managed it. I wasn't quite sure what to expect because people had told me that it wasn't the same as it used to be. Apparently, it's become much more touristy recently, but I didn't see any evidence of that. What did strike me was how confusing it is. Half the time I didn't know where I was and getting from A to B was always problematic. I normally have a good sense of direction, but I was always getting lost there. Once I did get to where I was trying to go, it was worth it, though.

Speaker 5: People always talk about what a marvellous place it is, and so eventually I decided to go and see for myself. It has the reputation of being a place you never forget, and lots of people say it's their favourite city. But, having been there, I can't see what all the fuss is about. Sure, the places that you see pictures of all the time, or that you see in films, are impressive enough, but I've seen better. It's a pleasant enough place, and it's certainly popular with tourists – there were plenty of them there – but I don't think it really deserves all the praise people give it.

In the exam you will hear the recording twice. To listen again now, go to the beginning of the track.

That is the end of Part Three. Now turn to Part Four.

You will hear an interview with someone who is involved in the music business. For questions 24–30, choose the best answer, A, B or C. You now have one minute to look at Part Four.

Interviewer: My next guest is James Hyland, the young Irish entrepreneur, who has been behind all sorts of music projects. The latest is Bubble TV, a music channel without advertising breaks. James, welcome.

James: Hi.

Interviewer: You're 23 now, but you launched yourself into the music world while you were still at school, didn't you? You were a very young starter!

James: Yes, I was 12 when I started my own radio station in my house. I played music I liked. The station was called Happiness. Not a good name I know, but I was young. I would have been happy if it had been just the neighbours listening, but it soon became clear that I'd attracted a lot of fans and I was invited to play at events. I ploughed all the money I made from that back into the station. It got very big and I got noticed.

Interviewer: Weren't people amazed when they found out you were 12?

James: Yes, but they were far more amazed when they discovered that I was organizing concerts by some of the biggest bands on the British music scene when I was just 16. That also attracted a lot of jealous rivalry. At 12 people are pleased for you, people are happy and encourage you, but when you're just a little older and running a successful business, it can be more of a threat.

Interviewer: So how did your career in music progress as you got older?

James: When I was 16, I started working with a local radio station. I didn't stay too long as I didn't like having a boss. But I didn't just complain and carry on going into work. I ditched the job and set up my own studio at my home in Cork, in southern Ireland, and began producing commercials from there. Along the way, I'd already started promoting well-known bands. I managed to bring in some fantastic acts to play at festivals and concerts in Ireland.

Interviewer: Now not so long ago, you launched the Bubble TV channel, a 24-hour all-music channel with no advertising breaks, aimed at teenagers. James, you seem to be the sort of person who's too busy to be the couch potato type, but the idea came from watching TV, didn't it?

James: Yes, I was flicking through all the channels and noticed there were so many of them but only three dedicated to music. And there weren't any exclusively British channels – most were from the US with British commercials. I hate ad breaks, they interrupt whatever you're watching and spoil the mood, so I decided not to have any. However, I should point out that Bubble TV has sponsored segments, so companies are involved. But the sponsorship doesn't get in the way, you have to look for a change in the background logo during programmes to notice it.

Interviewer: Is it just music and nothing else?

James: Although it's mainly music, we have three presenters, who do slots called Juice. They interview bands and go to gigs and festivals. And bands can't just promote their new song or whatever, it's got to be fun. They have to spill the juice – the gossip – in just three-minute slots! It has to be entertaining.

Interviewer: Now, you're constantly coming up with fresh ideas. Do you sleep with a notebook by the bed in case you dream up a best-selling idea in your sleep?

James: Absolutely. I text myself with my ideas as I have them, then each day I go through my texts to see what ideas I have sent myself.

Interviewer: So what's next?

James: Aah, I have several ideas ... but I'm not telling you!

Interviewer: OK, fair enough! Well, finally, have you got any tips for would-be entrepreneurs listening now?

James: Don't give up at the first sign of hardship. I've had my fingers burnt and lost money through some of my schemes in the past, but I've never let it get me down. I've had setbacks – but you can't dwell on them. You just move on.

Interviewer: James, thanks.

James: You're welcome.

In the exam you will hear the recording twice. To listen again now, go to the beginning of the track.

That is the end of Part Four.

TEST 2

Part One.
You will hear people talking in eight different situations.
For questions 1–8, choose the best answer, A, B or C.

ONE.
You hear part of an interview with a sportsman.

Interviewer: There's been talk of you being picked for the national team again. Is it hard for you to put that to the back of your mind during games, when you know that the national coach could be watching?

Sportsman: Playing for your country is as big as it gets, and it'd be great to do that again. But at the same time you have to worry about the job on the day, and that's playing for your club. I've learned over the years that your focus should be on the game you're playing in and nothing else. *repeat extract 1*

TWO.
You hear the introduction to a radio programme.

Presenter: Now, what do you do if you want to know what the weather is going to be like? You probably turn on the television or look on the Internet. But meteorology is a relatively recent science, and not so long ago people, especially farmers, had to rely on their own knowledge of the seasons. And no season was more important than spring. Many different rhymes and sayings were used for predicting the weather, and each month had its own sayings. *repeat extract 2*

THREE.
You hear a man talking about reading aloud to children.

Man: It doesn't really matter what you read to kids, they appreciate anything. I've been reading a book about history to my seven-year-old. He doesn't understand a word of it, but insists on having it every night. Having said that, it does make a huge difference if you can find a book that you all enjoy together. My favourite is a series of short stories about a mad inventor who creates ridiculous machines. It's great to be able to read something that genuinely makes your children laugh. *repeat extract 3*

FOUR.
You hear someone talking about work.

Man: So that's it. After all the months of worrying about it and discussing it with other people, I've finally done it. To be honest, I'm not sure how I feel. A bit anxious about the future, sure, because I really don't know how things are going to go. But I simply had to get out. You can't go on putting up with the sort of things I had to put up with. I still can't help thinking that it shouldn't have come to this. But it did, and I've dealt with it and it's time now to start looking ahead. *repeat extract 4*

FIVE.
You hear someone talking about his childhood.

Man: When I was a kid, I was always jumping out of windows and things and climbing trees. I had numerous injuries from things like that. Also, I went through a phase of wearing all my clothes back to front. Even to this day I don't know why I did it. In fact, I occasionally still do. I put my clothes on back to front and just sit there on my own because it reminds me of when I was a kid. *repeat extract 5*

SIX.
You hear someone talking about something that happened at a party.

Man: Yes, it was completely unexpected. I had no idea he felt so strongly about it. I mean, as far as I'm concerned I just made an innocent comment and he suddenly went mad. He was shouting at me and pointing his finger and I thought at one point he might even get violent. How silly. He just succeeded in making a complete fool of himself. Everyone else was looking terribly worried but I thought it was all highly entertaining. Some of those insults he was shouting at me – so ridiculous. I expect he'll apologize eventually but I really don't care. *repeat extract 6*

SEVEN.
You hear part of a talk about blues music.

Woman: Of course, without blues, you simply wouldn't have any of the various forms of popular music that have swept the world over the past few decades. Rock'n'roll, soul, rap, hip-hop – they all owe their existence to the style of music that was created in a small part of the Deep South of the US – the Mississippi Delta. The musicians who developed the style were all more or less totally unknown outside their own area, although fortunately they made plenty of recordings that are still available today if you want to find out more. And you should, if you want to find out where a lot of today's music came from. *repeat extract 7*

EIGHT.

You hear someone on the radio talking about a website for consumers.

Man: This is the first place to go if you need information about your rights as a consumer. It has tips on dealing with dodgy workmen, faulty goods, shopping safely online and avoiding scams. It's relatively easy to navigate your way around it, has a useful links section and will help you get in touch with telephone advisers. It will not, however, take up individual cases.
repeat extract 8

That is the end of Part One. Now turn to Part Two.

You will hear a radio reporter talking about indoor skydiving. For questions 9–18, complete the sentences with a word or short phrase. You now have 45 seconds to look at Part 2.

Reporter: OK, now we come to our regular spot on extreme sports, and this week I've been trying out something called indoor skydiving. It's the same as skydiving – jumping from an aeroplane and freefalling through the air without opening your parachute for some time – except that you do it in an indoor wind tunnel. And there's no plane, and no parachute, and, so I was told, no danger! So it gives you a taste of doing an extreme sport, but it isn't quite so extreme.

I went to an adventure sports centre called Runway, which has a vertical wind tunnel – a tunnel that gets filled with air. The air is provided by four enormous industrial fans of a kind that usually provide air for underground systems. These fans produce a column of air that rushes through the tunnel from below at more than 160 kilometres per hour. When you're in the tunnel, you float on this air. The machine has been described as being like an enormous hairdryer. It allows you to fly as if you had fallen from a plane, but you are only two metres off the ground.

Although this might sound a bit scary and dangerous, in fact it's completely safe. There are bars across the top of the tunnel to stop you flying off up and out of the tunnel. The tunnel is four metres wide and has glass walls. The only small problem you might have is that you keep bashing into these walls. But you're not really going to hurt yourself a lot by doing this – the only injuries you are likely to get are sore elbows and knees. There really is no danger involved and you don't need to be a strong, fit person to use the tunnel. In fact, it's so safe that the centre is open to anyone over the age of four. In America, where the idea was invented by the military in 1994, pensioners in their eighties regularly have a go.

Now, let me tell you about my experience of it. When I got there I watched the training instructors running through their routine. They were doing all sorts of moves in the tunnel, such as 'barrel rolls', something they call 'helicopters' – spinning on their heads in mid-air, and back flips. Watching them do all that before I went into the tunnel left me feeling a little anxious, even though I knew the tunnel was safe. And the roar of the electric motors that power the fans, like a plane taking off and so loud you need ear-plugs, added to my fear.

So I must admit that I was pretty nervous as I waited for my turn to get started. Like all beginners, I was given a couple of two-minute sessions in the tunnel, which seems short, but since the average freefall from a plane lasts only one minute, you realize it is more than plenty. Held down by my instructor, I floated in the position I was told to keep to, with my hands out in front of me as if I was 'holding a ball of air', for the whole session. The only time he had to correct me was on the occasions I threatened to fly out of reach or, as if by instinct, disappear out of the entry-exit door.

Even though it didn't last for long, I found the experience really exciting and great fun. In fact the person who came up with the idea and set up the centre calls it a 'smile machine', because nobody can go into the tunnel without smiling.

I would certainly recommend it to anyone who likes a bit of adventure. It's just like real skydiving, except that you don't have the view – or the expense! And it's good both for beginners and extreme skydivers. In fact, in some places it has developed into its own sport, known as body flying. There are already competitions in that sport.

Now, if you want to find out more about the wind tunnel, ... (fade)

In the exam you will hear the recording twice. To listen again now, go to the beginning of the track.

That is the end of Part Two. Now turn to Part Three.

You will hear five different people talking about the reasons why they became very successful. For questions 19–23, choose from the list A–H the reason each person gives for their success. Use the letters only once. There are three extra letters which you do not need to use. You now have thirty seconds to look at Part Three.

Speaker 1: I just fell into my television career really, there was no grand scheme. I guess it was all a case of simply being in the right place at the right time. I got my first job by pure chance and then one job offer followed another. I didn't set out to get where I am today and I'm sure there are plenty of people who could do the job as well as, if not better than, me. People tell me they like what I do, and that's great, but I'd probably be just as happy if the whole thing hadn't happened.

Speaker 2: When I started the company, the market was wide open really and hardly anyone was doing what I was doing. Actually, the product I was offering in the early days wasn't all that good, but there wasn't much to compare it with, so it did OK. The fact is, it was a good idea and in business there's no substitute for a good idea. I'm not necessarily a brilliant businessman in terms of strategy and things like that and sometimes I'm not sure what to do next. But I did have that great idea, so I've made my own luck.

Speaker 3: My personal feeling is that in show business, talent will always get its reward. Even if you have to struggle on for years – which, thankfully I didn't have to do – if you've got what it takes, you'll make it. Someone will spot you and give you a part if you're good enough, and that's exactly what happened to me. I've never really had to work at it, it just seems to be something I was born with. I've never thought of doing anything else, and fortunately I've never had to.

Speaker 4: There was no shortage of advice when I started my career as a singer. People told me how I should look, what sort of songs I should sing, all sorts of things. But I ignored them all, and I'm glad I did because I've been proved right. I had it all worked out from the very beginning, every detail of what I was going to do and how I was going to do it and it's all gone very smoothly. I knew what suited me and what would be popular and I've followed my instincts on that. I haven't had to struggle at all, everything's gone very well.

Speaker 5: To get to the top in my sport I've had to make the most of what I've got. I may not be the most talented player there's ever been but I've put a tremendous amount of effort in to be as good as I can be. All along there have been people making comments about how I'm not good enough, but that's just made me try even harder. And I've exceeded my ambitions really – I only wanted to be a good club player and I never imagined I'd make it into the national side.

In the exam you will hear the recording twice. To listen again now, go to the beginning of the track.

That is the end of Part Three. Now turn to Part Four.

You will hear part of a radio interview with a woman called Tania Wade about taking up running as a regular activity. For questions 24–30, choose the best answer, A, B or C. You now have one minute to look at Part Four.

Interviewer: Now Tania, you didn't even own a pair of running shoes until you were in your twenties, did you?

Tania: No, that's right. After a childhood and youth spent avoiding physical activity and sport at all costs, I am now, a decade and a half on, fitter and healthier than ever, and have completed more than 100 races, including ten marathons. And through my running I have gained a wonderful sense of independence, greater confidence, discipline and focus, a sanctuary from daily stresses and some great friendships. I can't quite remember what it was that first motivated me to go running – but whatever it was, I'm thankful for it now.

Interviewer: For people who don't go running, how would you sum up the main advantages for them if they do take it up?

Tania: I would say to them: you'll find that no other exercise variety gets results as fast as running. Give it a go and I promise you three things. Firstly, every muscle from the waist down will become stronger, tighter and firmer while excess body fat will be sent marching. Secondly, you'll feel great about yourself. You'll have more energy, you'll feel alert and focused and you'll experience a real sense of accomplishment as you gradually become fitter and stronger. And finally, you'll find that running is very easy to fit into your life.

Interviewer: What, easier than other sports and physical activities?

Tania: Yes, unlike that exercise class, you don't have to be somewhere dead on six o'clock, unlike swimming you don't have to get to the pool before closing time, unlike tennis or squash, you don't have to rely on someone else to make it happen. You can go for fifteen minutes at lunchtime, or grab half an hour in the morning. You can hit the city streets or head for the park. All in all you can make running fit into your life without too much effort.

Interviewer: But it's not for everyone is it? Some people might say 'I'm too old' or 'I'm too overweight' or 'I'm too embarrassed' to take up running?

Tania: Yes, these are worries that people often reveal when they are faced with the prospect of taking up exercise. Well, I can't categorically say to each and every one of those people 'no, you're not' but I can tell you that I know people who have become runners in their 40s, 50s and 60s, and only wish they'd done it sooner. I know people who've gone out running in the streets in bad weather and risked funny looks from passers-by, and now wouldn't give it up for the world. After all, one of the greatest pleasures in life is overcoming fears and obstacles.

Interviewer: What advice would you give people who are thinking of taking it up?

Tania: Well, I do have one warning. To get the benefits, you have to approach running with patience and respect. Try to achieve too much too soon and you'll end up aching, disillusioned and possibly even injured. The golden rule is to start slow, and progress one step at a time. Some people improve quicker than others, too, so don't compare your progress to anyone else's.

Interviewer: Now, what about running technique? What advice would you give on that?

Tania: Well, if you remember only one thing, remember to relax! Unclench your fists, relax your jaw and keep your shoulders loose. Think 'up' before moving forwards. This helps you stay light on your feet, and makes you run tall rather than sinking into the hips. Remember to use your arms. Picture them as pistons, propelling you forwards. Keep them bent to roughly 90 degrees. It's particularly important to think about your arms if you hit an incline – increasing the arm effort will help you get up the hill more easily.

Interviewer: OK, and what about breathing while you run? What's your advice there?

Tania: Well, despite all the theories people have about breathing in through your nose and out through your mouth, or breathing in time with your footfall, I recommend just getting the oxygen in whatever way feels most comfortable to you.

Interviewer: Right, now tell me about the Get Running programme that you're involved with …

In the exam you will hear the recording twice. To listen again now, go to the beginning of the track.

That is the end of Part Four.

TEST 3

Part One
You will hear people talking in eight different situations. For questions 1–8, choose the best answer, A, B or C.

ONE.
You hear part of an interview with a pop singer.

Interviewer: I hear that you missed a concert you were supposed to do in Germany recently. How did that happen?

Female singer: Well, I just lost my passport. I couldn't find it anywhere in my house. Obviously, I would say that it wasn't my fault, but, well, it wasn't my fault! I just assumed that our tour manager had it. But he didn't have it. He normally keeps it for me when I'm travelling for concerts and I don't know how it got lost. I've had to get a replacement one. *repeat extract 1*

TWO.
You hear part of a radio programme for young people.

Woman: We've got an email from Beth, who says, 'My family hasn't got a car, and we walk or cycle everywhere. My friends laugh at me because they all have cars. What should I do?' Well, Beth, there is a lot to be said for not having a car unless you really need one. In fact, it would be much better for the environment if fewer people had cars. Your so-called friends are unkind to judge you on what you have or don't have. People like this are very materialistic and not worth bothering with. And think how much fitter and healthier than them you'll be because of all the exercise you get! *repeat extract 2*

THREE.
You hear a radio presenter talking about a book.

Presenter: The country's most talented young writers have seen their hard work come to fruition with the publication of the very first Young Writer's Year Book. Thousands of children aged nine to seventeen submitted their stories and poems to win a chance to be published. The successful entries have now been published in this wonderful book. Sad, surprising, witty, frightening, insightful, wise and full of potential, this is a deliciously fresh collection by the best-selling authors of the future. *repeat extract 3*

FOUR.
You hear someone talking on the phone.

Man: Look, I don't see why this has to become a big thing. The fact is that our ideas aren't that far apart and I'm sure if we just have a reasonable chat about the situation, we can sort things out. What do you think?

I mean, it makes no sense to have a big row about it, and I know that neither of us wants to do that. I'm sure we can work something out that suits both of us, so let's do it now. I'm willing to compromise if you are. *repeat extract 4*

FIVE.

You hear someone talking to an assistant at a box office.

Man: I know it's very late but I really would appreciate it if you could help me out. You see, something's come up at the last minute and we won't be able to make it tonight. Of course, I've already paid for the tickets and I ordered the best seats. I was looking forward to it so I'm annoyed that I'm going to have to miss the show. I know you've got your rules about not giving refunds but couldn't you make an exception for me? *repeat extract 5*

SIX.

You hear someone talking about her personality.

Woman: I just don't seem to have any patience. I know it's not a great thing, and I really ought to be able to stay calm more instead of losing my temper, but I just can't help myself. When someone gets on my nerves I just have to tell them, it just comes straight out of my mouth. There's no excuse for it, I know I ought to have more self-control. And sometimes I do try, honestly, but it just never seems to work. *repeat extract 6*

SEVEN.

You hear two people talking.

Man: I haven't seen you for a while.

Woman: No, I've been really busy. I've had a couple of assignments I had to do for college and they've taken up all my time.

Man: Oh, we don't have those.

Woman: Well, I've done them now, so I've got a bit more time. Do you fancy a game some time?

Man: Sure. I'll book a court for us. How about tomorrow evening?

Woman: Sounds good. Actually, that reminds me that I have to renew my membership. I'll do it while I'm there tomorrow.

Man: Yes, I did it last month. Shall I pick you up at home?

Woman: That'd be great.

Man: OK, I'll come round for you at about 7.

Woman: Excellent. *repeat extract 7*

EIGHT.

You hear a local radio presenter talking about a competition.

Presenter: OK, here are the details of our competition to find the best amateur chef in the region. To enter, you have to send in a main course and dessert recipe with ingredients that cost less than £10 per person.

From the recipes sent in, we'll draw up a shortlist of ten finalists, and they'll be asked to come along to Pandora's Restaurant and cook their recipes for the panel of judges and paying customers, with the assistance of the restaurant's chef. The judges will then choose three people to go forward to the final. The final three will be asked to create a three-course recipe and cook it at the restaurant for the judges and paying customers. The judges will then choose the winner. *repeat extract 8*

That is the end of Part One.

Now turn to Part Two.

You will hear someone introducing a conference for the organizers of music festivals. For questions 9–18, complete the sentences with a word or short phrase. You now have 45 seconds to look at Part 2.

Conference Organizer: Hello and welcome everybody, it's great to see so many of you here. The aim of this conference is to give you some information and ideas that may be useful for your own festivals and also for people to exchange information and experiences with each other. I'll just briefly run through what we'll be covering at the conference today.

In the first session, we're going to look at festival sites and some of the issues involved. We'll be looking at some of the problems that can arise with land owners after you've made a deal to use their property for your festival. During this session, a legal expert will explain how you can avoid such problems by making sure that they are covered in the contract you sign. Of course, some unforeseen problems always come up, but it is possible to prevent the most common ones.

Another area we'll look at in this session on sites is the question of facilities. People judge festivals not just by the music, of course, but also by how good and how plentiful these are. On the panel for this session, we have representatives from firms that supply toilets, catering and other services, and you'll have a chance to find out about these services and exchange views about them. Finally, in this session, we'll be looking at the impact of the weather on festivals and what you can do to plan for that in terms of indoor or undercover stages and other areas.

The second session will focus on the entertainment you provide, principally the music. We'll be discussing the various ways that festival organizers choose artists, including the role played by agents when it comes to booking acts. We'll also look at how best to give local musicians a chance to play at your festival. One possible approach that has become more popular in recent years is to hold a competition, with the winning band or artist getting a slot at the festival. We'll be discussing how desirable these competitions are – most of them use some kind of voting procedure involving the general public rather than a panel of experts, so the result might not always be the one you were hoping for. We'll also be getting your views on whether this approach is a good way to generate publicity for your event.

In the third session we'll look at staffing and in particular how to go about getting volunteers to work at your festival. What can you offer them in return to ensure that you get enough people in those roles? And what roles at a festival definitely require professionals? One issue that comes up time and time again is that of security – how much of it do you need and what kind? We've got a representative from a firm that specializes in festivals, and he'll be giving you his thoughts on how festival organizers could improve in this area.

In the final session, we'll be focusing on the question of promoting your festival to maximize attendance. One key topic we'll be covering is social networking and its effectiveness, as well as more targeted marketing, for example advertisements on websites connected with the kind of music at your festival. Pricing is a key factor in making your event cost-effective; however you need to avoid putting off potential customers by charging too much. Offering discounts for advance tickets is very common and we'll consider how effective that can be.

OK, now, before we start the first session ....

In the exam you will hear the recording twice. To listen again now, go to the beginning of the track.

That is the end of Part Two. Now turn to Part Three.

You will hear five different people talking about what they discovered when they read autobiographies by famous people. For questions 19–23, choose from the list A–H what each person says that they discovered. Use the letters only once. There are three extra letters which you do not need to use. You now have 30 seconds to look at Part Three.

Speaker 1: What struck me most was just how arrogant the man is! I mean, he's a fine actor and I really like everything he's been in – that's why I bought the book. But that doesn't mean that his opinions on politics and the world really matter. He seems to think they do, and that because he's been in a few successful films, people should listen to his views on everything and take them seriously. Actually, he talks a lot of rubbish about all that and that really irritated me. I wanted to read about his early life and struggles, how he got to the top and all that, but he hardly mentions that, or anything about his private life. It's really put me off him.

Speaker 2: I got the book because a friend recommended it, not because I was particularly interested in the man. In fact, from his public image on TV, I thought he was a ghastly person. Self-important, fiercely ambitious and not at all likeable is how he appears to me. So I was very surprised to find that he isn't actually like that at all, that's just for public consumption. In reality, he's a decent person who puts family and friendship first and he comes across as the sort of person you could have a pleasant chat with. He's certainly gone up in my estimation.

Speaker 3: His family seem to have played a very important part in his career, and he talks about how much help they gave him in the early days, paying for coaches and taking him to tournaments all over the place. But he admits that after he made it to the top, he didn't treat them at all well. He talks about how much pressure he was under once he became a champion and how he struggled to deal with all the attention from the media and fans. We always saw him smiling in victory, but he says that he was really horrible to the people who were closest to him. It just shows that appearances can be deceptive.

Speaker 4: Of course, people always say that comedians are actually very sad people but that doesn't seem to be the case here. With him it seems to be very much 'what you see is what you get'. The book's full of really funny stories, and he makes fun of everything, from some of the things that happened during his childhood to the big issues in the world today. He seems to have come from a very peculiar family and his descriptions of them are really amusing. You get the impression that there is no difference between his personality on stage and on screen and what he's like when he's not performing.

Speaker 5: It's quite an uplifting story, really, a real 'rags to riches' one. Of course I knew all about his enormous success as a businessman, but I didn't know anything about his background. It certainly wasn't a privileged one, and he seems to have grown up in poverty with a family who didn't really care about him at all. The way he describes his childhood, it's hard to imagine how it could have been any worse. So the fact that he managed to go from that to such incredible success and wealth makes for a really interesting story. You don't get much of an idea of the real person, but the story is great.

In the exam you will hear the recording twice. To listen again now, go to the beginning of the track.

That is the end of Part Three. Now turn to Part Four.

You will hear an interview with someone whose daughters are appearing in a show in London. For questions 24–30, choose the best answer, A, B or C. You now have one minute to look at Part Four.

Interviewer: I'm talking to Jackie Gould, who's a very proud mother. Both of her daughters – Olivia, aged 12, and Alicia, seven – are currently appearing on the stage of the world-famous London Palladium theatre, in the musical *The Sound of Music*. Olivia and Alicia survived six auditions to be picked from 1,000 hopefuls for the group of seven children playing the Von Trapp family in the show. So how did it all come about?

Jackie: Well, until last year, the idea of them appearing at the London Palladium would have been unthinkable for our family. Things started to happen when Olivia auditioned for a production of the show *Annie* at the local theatre. She auditioned for the chorus and, by chance, got the leading role instead.

Interviewer: That's a very big role, the leading one in *Annie*, isn't it?

Jackie: Yes, for *Annie*, Olivia had to learn more than 200 lines. She was on stage for most of the two-hour show. It was a big script, and I decided that we'd do ten pages a night. After memorizing it, I gave her a random line. She would have to tell me what the next line was. She picked it all up even better than her homework.

Interviewer: And she did well in the part, presumably?

Jackie: She was great in the part. Everyone was astonished by her performance, including us. She had always been very shy, and she suddenly came out of her shell. We found that she could really sing. A member of the stage management team for the show was taking over a local agency and asked her to sign up. So then she had an agent to represent her and try to get roles for her.

Interviewer: OK, so what happened next?

Jackie: Well, Olivia was turned down for a part in the musical *Mary Poppins*. She reached the last ten for the role of Jane Banks. She didn't get the part and was distraught. But she quickly picked herself up and then we took both children to the Palladium auditions for *The Sound of Music*.

Interviewer: What was that like?

Jackie: Well, we arrived for the auditions at 8.30 a.m., as instructed, only to find a huge crowd ahead of us. Eventually, more than 1,000 children turned up. They said at first that they could only see 230 kids. We were at about number 250 and, with a visit to our local festival planned for the next day, we couldn't come back. We begged them to see our daughters and eventually they agreed.

Interviewer: And it went well?

Jackie: Both girls sang 'Over The Rainbow' for the producers and a week later they were told they had passed the initial hurdle. Their first call-back involved singing the harmonies for the title theme, as well as the song 'The Lonely Goatherd' from the show. I helped them rehearse by playing the tunes on our old upright piano in our dining room. They really worked hard and decided that for all auditions they would wear what they felt were their lucky clothes. Alicia had on a skirt and top and some dolly shoes. Olivia wore three-quarter length trousers, a stripy T-shirt and dolly shoes.

Interviewer: So they got through that audition?

Jackie: Yes, and for the next one they had to read some poetry, and eventually they got to the sixth and final one. It was all quite tense at the last audition. Alicia was already set to appear in a local show, so she was not openly worried, and Olivia joked that if she was rejected she could still sell programmes at the show. I impressed upon them that they need not worry if they were rejected, as much depended on whether their faces fitted, or they were the right height. I told them it was all down to luck.

Interviewer: But they passed, and now they're in the show. They must be thrilled.

Jackie: Yes. But it hasn't gone to their heads. I've told them both they're very lucky, and if all fails, life will go on as usual. They're both quite quiet, not show-offs, and they've got their feet firmly on the ground.

Interviewer: Well, wish them good luck from me.

Jackie: I will. Thanks.

In the exam you will hear the recording twice. To listen again now, go to the beginning of the track.

That is the end of Part Four.

TEST 4

Part One
You will hear people talking in eight different situations. For questions 1–8, choose the best answer, A, B or C.

ONE.
You hear someone talking on a radio programme.

Woman: Fresh lime soda is made by the side of the road in Calcutta, India. Citrus drinks are popular all over India but fresh lime soda is a speciality in Calcutta. Stallholders set up early in the morning, making the drink with fresh limes, soda water, sugar, a pinch of salt and freshly ground cumin. In hot weather, the body loses a lot of its salt through perspiration, so salty drinks, especially those with lime juice, are very refreshing. Limes grow easily in India and are used in numerous recipes. *repeat extract 1*

TWO.

You hear someone talking about people who travel a lot when they're young.

Man: Of course these days there are lots of young people who spend a period of time travelling all over the world. We couldn't do that when I was younger – you couldn't get to all these places so easily and we didn't have the time or the money. But I don't feel like I've missed out at all. I mean, what do they actually see and learn? It seems to me that they just do it for the sake of it, as if they're just ticking places off on a list. They just do it because it's what people do. They can't be bothered to find out about the people or their culture. They just want to talk about where they've been when they get back. *repeat extract 2*

THREE.

You hear an advertisement for a course.

Woman: Our Gym Instructor course will help you gain the skills and knowledge you need to get the best out of people and help them reach their fitness goals. On successful completion of the course, you'll be able to take the practical assessment test to prove that you've reached a recognized standard in working with people of different fitness levels and abilities. As well as studying anatomy and physiology, you'll learn about the importance of customer care and correct exercise technique. *repeat extract 3*

FOUR.

You hear part of a radio interview.

Interviewer: Do you ever add your own bits to a scene?

Man: I think with everything you do, you have the basic structure, but you do your best to explore it as much as possible while you're shooting a film. If you do something on the spur of the moment, it can be fun. You see the reactions all around. People panic for a second.

Interviewer: A lot of your characters have been pretty strange, haven't they?

Man: Are you saying I'm weird? Well, I think everyone's nuts, I really do. The strangest people in the world are the ones who are super-serious. They're probably crazier than any of the guys I've played. *repeat extract 4*

FIVE.

You hear part of a radio report about car drivers.

Reporter: The meanings of symbols on dashboards are beyond the grasp of many drivers, a survey shows. Almost half of women and a third of men surveyed by the Automobile Association could not correctly identify symbols for frequently-used functions or basic warning lights. Researchers found that nearly 40 per cent of women and 28 per cent of men were unable to correctly identify the warning lamp for the main beam headlight. Two thirds of women could not correctly identify the front windscreen washer and wipe symbol and one in five admitted that they had no idea what it signified. *repeat extract 5*

SIX.

You turn on the radio and hear part of a programme.

Woman: It would be very interesting to find out what he was trying to achieve on this latest CD, because it's totally different from his previous ones. He's given several interviews since it came out but he doesn't seem to want to discuss the thinking behind this extraordinary change of style. Of course, the fans will make their views clear – they'll either stick with him despite the sudden change or they just won't buy it. Personally, I think it's a very effective and powerful set of songs and he deserves praise for not just sticking with his tried and tested formula. It's certainly the best of the releases we've looked at so far. *repeat extract 6*

SEVEN.

You hear part of a radio play.

Man: Look, I know you're upset, but let's not ruin the whole evening over this.

Woman: That's easy for you to say. You're not the one who's been insulted.

Man: I know, but just try to forget it. Let's go for our meal, just as we planned it and try to enjoy ourselves. I have booked a table after all.

Woman: No, I just can't face it. Turn around and take me back. I'm really not in the mood.

Man: Well, I'm hungry.

Woman: Go on your own, then. But drop me off first. I just want to be on my own. *repeat extract 7*

EIGHT.

You hear a woman talking about running.

Woman: At school and college, I used to belong to an athletics club and enthusiastically took part in cross-country races. But then for years I didn't really do any exercise. Then, eighteen months ago, I decided to get fit and stay fit, and I rediscovered the joys of running. I started training and was soon hooked on running again. I got a colleague to join me and she caught the running bug so badly that she even joined an athletics club! Seeing each other every day at work and discussing running kept us both motivated and I found it surprisingly easy to stick to my schedule of training in the gym and going out for road runs. *repeat extract 8*

That is the end of Part One. Now turn to Part Two.

You will hear an announcement about a competition. For questions 9–18, complete the sentences with a word or short phrase. You now have 45 seconds to look at Part 2.

Woman: So, are you thinking about that idea again? That absolute money-spinner, the ultimate business brainchild that could change your fortunes and transform your life forever? No, you think, it's impossible. People like you should stick to dreaming. But what if you were given a real chance to change your life and achieve that goal? How would you react if the support you need suddenly landed in your lap? Not in the form of a loan – but free. Well, now's your chance. In this competition, we're offering £100,000 to a budding entrepreneur. and there are no obligations other than that you have to use the money to follow through your idea. All you have to do is convince us that your plan is worth backing. The £100,000 prize is to help pay for your financial commitments while you pursue your goal.

The competition is open to a variety of ideas and people. Perhaps you have a particular skill that you know could be put to more effective use in a different sector or country. Perhaps, given the right backing, you could change hundreds of lives. Are you an engineer with an idea that could transform sanitation and bring clean water to Africa? Or an architect with a vision that could solve the problems in Britain's inner cities? Or are you a farmer who could teach the world's poorest people how to grow crops in the worst conditions? If you are any of these, you could win the competition and the prize money.

Here are the details for entering. If you phone, after leaving your name and address, you will have up to one minute to pitch your idea. If you choose to email, you will have to pitch your idea in no more than 100 words. There are three categories of entry, and you will have to choose one of them. The first category is for those with an innovative idea for a business offering a new product or service. The second is for those who plan to learn new skills by taking a course such as an MBA. The third is for those who want to use their skills to support a socially-responsible project. The winner will be chosen from across all three categories.

Now, there are some other very important details if you are thinking of going in for the competition. Only one entry per person is allowed – multiple entries are not permitted. If you make a mistake while delivering your pitch, you will not be allowed to call back and leave another entry. We suggest that you practise delivering your pitch before phoning. If it helps, write down a script and read that. And remember, you can't go over the time limit.

Our judges will be looking for a number of qualities when they make their decision. The best idea will have big potential and demonstrate a great deal of innovation. The judges will want to be sure that the idea, if it was carried out, would change the life of the entrant, and preferably the lives of others. Entrants must be able to demonstrate great passion for their project, with thought having been given to how it could be put into practice. The top 100 will then be whittled down to 10, who will be invited to present their ideas in person to a panel of judges. The winner will then be announced.

In the exam you will hear the recording twice. To listen again now, go to the beginning of the track.

That is the end of Part Two. Now turn to Part Three.

You will hear five different people talking about how they felt when they received an award. For questions 19–23, choose from the list A–H how each person felt. Use the letters only once. There are three extra letters which you do not need to use. You now have 30 seconds to look at Part Three.

Speaker 1: When I won the Best Actor award it was an extraordinary moment. There had been so many occasions when I'd thought I might win an award, only to find that someone else got it instead. So when I finally got it I was thrilled. It was a fantastic personal achievement but in fact the main thing in my mind was all the people who had helped me along the way. I thought about all of them and all the help they'd given me. I knew that without them I would never have won it. And I mentioned as many of them as I could in the time available.

Speaker 2: I guess that being voted Footballer of the Year went to my head. All I could think about was how well I'd done. Me, the best! I thought back to the early years of my career, which weren't so great and I felt fantastic. And it was all thanks to my own efforts, not because anyone had handed me anything on a plate. It had been a long, hard journey but I'd finally made it to the very top. I suppose it made me a bit big-headed for a while, but I just felt so good about myself and what I'd managed to achieve.

Speaker 3: Everybody was expecting me to win the Writer of the Year award – I don't know why, there were plenty of other good contenders on the shortlist. Because everyone was predicting I'd win, I felt under pressure, as if it would be some kind of failure if I didn't win. It was a silly way to feel, I know, but I couldn't help it. So when my name was announced I was just glad that it was over and I had in fact won it. All the pressure came off me in a moment and I just felt like sitting down quietly rather than celebrating.

Speaker 4: These awards mean a lot in the music business and so winning the Best Singer award was a great honour. I'd worked so hard over the years and I'd spent so long getting nowhere that it was amazing to have achieved this recognition. I thought I'd be absolutely overcome with joy, but in fact the reverse happened. As I accepted the award, I was wondering if it would be all downhill from there. Would I be able to keep it up and stay at the top? Or would this be the high point, followed by a lot of low points? I couldn't put those thoughts out of my mind.

Speaker 5: I wasn't totally surprised when I got the Best Student award, because to be honest I felt that I deserved it. In fact, I'd put in so much effort to win it, doing far more work than anyone else, that I was completely worn out. It had been so important to me to win it that I'd dedicated myself completely to the task of winning it. So when I went up to collect it, I'd used up all my energy over the previous couple of weeks and was totally drained. I could barely put a few sentences together for my acceptance speech, though I managed to remember to thank a few people for their help.

In the exam you will hear the recording twice. To listen again now, go to the beginning of the track.

That is the end of Part Three. Now turn to Part Four.

You will hear an interview with someone who has started a magazine for children. For questions 24–30, choose the best answer, A, B or C. You now have one minute to look at Part Four.

Interviewer: It's tough maintaining a child's interest, but Kate Scarborough has had the experience to know what it's all about. Kate, you used to be a teacher, didn't you?

Kate: Yes, six years ago I had the idea that I wanted to do something for children, so I decided to be a primary school teacher. I have never been so tired as I was working as a teacher in a classroom. You just never stop. Working with children is so intensely exhausting, but it's also fantastic.

Interviewer: Well, today, we're sitting in your London office and talking about something very different – being the founder of *CY* magazine, a new magazine for children. Having worked in children's non-fiction publishing for 12 years before retraining as a primary school teacher, you certainly have the background to produce such a magazine.

Kate: Yes, well being a teacher I guess led me to the idea for *CY*. I felt that there was a gap in the market for a monthly publication that not only entertains and teaches children, but also satisfies their parents

too. And it was during my teaching days that I began preparing for *CY*. I talked to children about what they wanted. I then thought, if I was a child, what would I want, and as a parent, what would I want my children to be reading?

Interviewer: OK, now the outcome is a magazine that's filled with competitions, short stories, puzzles, and a cartoon strip. Flicking through the first issue, I'd say two things become apparent – enthusiasm and the language used.

Kate: Enthusiasm is incredibly important. When I was at school, it didn't matter what you were teaching children if you totally believed in it. When you give a bad lesson, you can see those blank faces looking back at you. I really hope I get that belief across, and that children find it entertaining and become interested in what's going on around them all the time.

Interviewer: How about the actual style of writing itself?

Kate: The whole brief to my writers was that they should approach it as if they are talking to intelligent people. Of course, you can't use some words because they would go above children's heads. But when I was doing my research, I put a number of texts in front of children. They are very perceptive – if they feel they are being talked down to, they see it. So it's all written in a direct way, rather than assuming you have to use a very childish style – the readers wouldn't like that.

Interviewer: Now, the age range for the magazine is stated as 7 to 12 years, but it's quite difficult to judge that, isn't it?

Kate: Yes, children develop at different rates. For some at 7 it will be difficult, but for others perfect. And when some hit 12 they become interested in totally different things. Parents will know whether or not it's right for their children.

Interviewer: Now a very interesting aspect of the magazine is its use of the Internet. Tell me about that.

Kate: Well, if children read something that interests them, by visiting the magazine's website they can learn much more about it. The reasons for this are rooted in my experiences at school. Take explorers as a subject. There are so many fantastic stories attached to them and all kinds of themes to raise excitement, but you can't spend a week teaching them that. So I wanted readers to be able to follow up a subject, in a way they may not be able to at school.

Interviewer: Now obviously, you want the magazine to be successful and profitable, I assume?

Kate: Yes, but ultimately, it isn't making a profit that's on my mind. I want to inspire children. If a child reads an article in the magazine on houses, for example, and they are inspired to go on to be an architect, that's great. It can be the tiniest thing that sparks a child off. From my point of view, I am trying to cover as much as I can so there's a chance of that little spark.

Interviewer: OK, now another aspect of the magazine

....

In the exam you will hear the recording twice. To listen again now, go to the beginning of the track.

That is the end of Part Four.